The
Red Wine
Companion
A CONNOISSEUR'S GUIDE
Michael Edwards

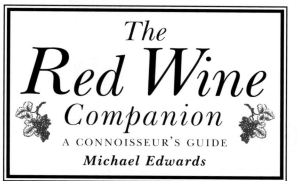

The
Red Wine
Companion
A CONNOISSEUR'S GUIDE

Michael Edwards

FIREFLY BOOKS

Dedication

For Dr. Teresa Challoner,
without whose help this book
would never have been written.

A FIREFLY BOOK

First published in Canada in 1998
by Firefly Books Ltd.
3680 Victoria Park Avenue
Willowdale, Ontario M2H 3KI

Published in the United States in 1998
by Firefly Books (U.S.) Inc.
P.O. Box 1338, Ellicott Station
Buffalo, New York 14205

Cataloguing in Publication Data
Edwards, Michael
The red wine companion

Includes index
ISBN 1-55209-256-9

I. Wine and Wine Making. I. Title
TP 543, E38 1998   641.2'223   C98-930458-2

This book was designed and produced by
Quintet Publishing Limited
6 Blundell Street
London N7 9BH

Creative Director: Richard Dewing
Art Director: Clare Reynolds
Designer: Ian Hunt
Senior Editor: Laura Sandelson
Editor: Donna Dailey
Photographer: Adrian Swift

Typeset in Great Britain by
Central Southern Typesetters, Eastbourne
Manufactured in Singapore by
Pica Colour Separation Overseas Private Limited
Printed in China by
Leefung-Asco Printers Trading Limited

TABLE OF CONTENTS

Introduction
6

Introduction

The ancient Greek poet Homer was perhaps the first writer to celebrate red wine, for his hero Achilles has an image of an idyllic vineyard full of black grapes painted on his trusty shield. This book is a celebration of great red wine, charting the progress of its making over the centuries, to the present where it is regarded as the most varied, yet essentially comforting beverage in the world.

This is a very personal selection from someone who has spent most of his working life poking around the cellars of wine growers. As a traditionalist, I look for balance and a sense of place, rather than power and technical wizardry, in my favorite wines. Wines should also have a complexity, even a touch of austerity, to make them great partners for food. Inevitably, greatness does not come cheap, but in assembling the directory, I have always tried to choose wines that are intrinsically good value for money.

HOW TO USE THE DIRECTORY

The wine estates and houses are categorized not by country or region, but by the style of the wines they make and the sort of producer they are. There are three style categories.

Classics: Usually internationally famous names, producers who make wine in classic non-interventionist way which is a very particular expression of the *terroir(s)* where the grapes are grown. The "Classics" are not all from Europe, let alone France; the New World classics are among the very best.

Benchmarkers: Producers, highly respected for making textbook examples of the wine of their *appellation*/region. Often innovators in winemaking techniques and masters of their craft, they are not necessarily household names, though they can be rejuvenated estates now returned to former glories.

Rising Stars: Self-explanatory. Particularly exciting producers who have appeared on the scene within the last 20 years and who are likely to produce tomorrow's classics.

Star ratings: All wines tasted have an overall rating between ★ (adequate) and ★★★★★ (outstanding, truly great).

PART ONE

THE *story of* RED WINE

A BRIEF HISTORY

It is impossible to say exactly where and when wine was first made, for unlike the inventions of distilling and brewing, winemaking is a natural process that, in principle, can happen without human intervention. A bunch of grapes falls from the vine, the skins split, the seeping juice comes into contact with airborne yeasts, and in a little while you have a wine of sorts. This phenomenon must have been observed by our earliest forebears, so it is conceivable that wine is as old as man himself, at least in those regions of the world where grapes grew wild.

Vitis vinifera, the species of vine from which most modern wine is made, is thought to have originated about 7500 BC in the Transcaucasian region of what is now Armenia and Georgia. by classical times, wine-bearing vines were grown in almost all

Stone carving of Bacchus, God of Wine.

countries bordering the Mediterranean littoral. The tomb paintings of the Pharaohs (c. 2000 BC) illustrate in meticulous detail each stage of the wine harvest in ancient Egypt, where, according to celebrated wine writer Hugh Johnson, "there were ... experts who discriminated between qualities of wine as confidently and professionally as a sherry shipper or Bordeaux broker of the twentieth century."

To the ancient Greeks, wine was a cornerstone of their remarkable culture and an essential part of daily living: in Homer's epic poem The *Iliad*, wine is always dark in color and his depiction of the essence of human life takes the form of an idyllic enclosed vineyard full of black grapes. Under the Mycenaens (c. 1600–1100 BC), Greek wine is believed to have been exported to Egypt, Syria, the Black Sea, Sicily, and southern Italy. Later, around 600 BC, Phocaean Greeks from Asia Minor founded the city of Massalia (Marseille) in the south of France, bringing the vine and the olive with them.

Wine was an integral part of Roman culture and made a major contribution to the imperial economy. The great Roman writers Pliny and Columella describe the chief vine varieties of the ancient world, but it is difficult to determine whether these were the forerunners of modern varieties because vine species have mutated frequently. Much more fun is the experience of tasting powerful southern Italian red wine from the Aglianico grape (reputedly of ancient Greek origin) by such fine modern producers as Mastroberardino of Avellino or the d'Angelo brothers in Basilicata.

The first French red wine of quality to command a high price outside its locality appears to have been a northern Rhone from first-century Vienne, later to become famous as Côte Rôtie ("The Roasted Slope"). The earliest vineyards of Bordeaux and Burgundy were probably planted in the third century; others in the Ile de France, Champagne, and the Loire Valley followed in the fourth and fifth centuries. After the fall of Rome, France, though nominally Christian, entered a dark pagan age that was to last for 300 years until the accession of Charlemagne to the Frankish throne. He colonized the whole of Germany, Lombardy, and even parts of Spain, unifying the whole into the Holy Roman Empire on Christmas Day 800. Under Charlemagne's stable rule, monastic communities flourished, and they developed the methods of vineyard tending and cellarwork so well that their principles are still broadly followed by some traditionalist wine producers.

BURGUNDY ... THE FIRST PERFECTIONISTS

The Cistercians were the *virtuosi* winemakers of the medieval world. Their story begins in 1112 when a young ascetic monk, Bernard de Fontaine, led a breakaway group of 30 novices from the Abbey of Cluny into a small new monastery at Citeaux, north of Beaune in Burgundy's Côte d'Or. The Cistercian Rule of Life was killing–an average monk's lifespan was 28 years–as the regime mainly consisted of many hours of stone-breaking work in a neglected vineyard. But by the time of St. Bernard's death in 1153, the Cistercians were making wine in almost every commune of the Côte d'Or, and much farther afield from the bases of 400 abbeys spread across Europe.

Tapestry from the sixteenth century illustrating the
wine-making process.

The Cistercians were model *vignerons*, studying the best vines,
making the wine with the greatest care, and advancing their art
with constant experimentation. Lalou Bize-Leroy, the outstanding
twentieth-century Burgundy producer, believes that the Cistercians
actually tasted the soil to distinguish one piece of land from
another, and they virtually invented the idea of the *cru*, or growth,
that is a homogeneous plot of land in a vineyard area that has an
individual flavor and style. So, thanks to the Church, their fame
spread throughout Europe. The Avignon popes in the fourteenth
century were particularly partial to Burgundy wines. Duke Philippe
the Bold of Burgundy was a great PR man for his wines: at a papal

conference in Bruges he offered the delegates as much French wine as they could drink, but only a sip of the rare red wine of Beaune.

The adage "drink less but better" is as old as the hills. But then fine red Burgundy has never been about rapid expansion on the grand scale; rather it is a story of a quest for the perfect expression of Pinot Noir in the remarkable soils of the Côte d'Or. Wine made in small amounts from tiny parcels is the name of the game, especially since the French Revolution of 1789 when the vineyards of Burgundy were broken up into tiny plots after the suppression of the monasteries and the liquidation of the aristocratic estates of the *ancien régime*.

Nineteenth century etching of a bordeaux grape harvest on
the left bank of the Gironde above Pauillac; the tower of
Château Latour is visible through the trees behind the river.

CLARET AND ENGLAND

Red Bordeaux wine has always been an Englishman's tipple, ever
since Gascony became an English possession on the union of King
Henry II and Eleanor of Aquitaine in 1154. "Claret," the English
pet name for red Bordeaux, comes from the French word *claire*
meaning light and clear, for the claret of the Middle Ages was more
pink than red and a wine for immediate drinking. King John, Henry
II's son, gave the merchants of Bordeaux their head in 1203 by
exempting them from the punitive tax on their wine exports and
within 50 years, 75 percent of the English royal household's needs
was coming from Bordeaux. In 1307, Edward II ordered the
equivalent of 1.15 million bottles of claret for his wedding!

Even after Gascony reverted to French rule at the end of the
Hundred Years' War, the Bordelais continued to ship claret to
England, though orders slowed as the practical Dutch came to
dominate the market with their taste for cheap dark wine at a
knockdown price. Claret remained a bulk commodity until the
advent of corks and glass in the 1630s; thereafter it had the
potential to be a fine wine capable of improving for several years in
an airtight bottle.

France

CALAIS

BELGIUM

LUXEMBOURG

GERMANY

Champagne

PARIS

STRASBOURG

Marne

Alsace

ORLEANS

Chablis

DIJON

Côtes de Beaune

Côtes de Nuits

SWITZERLA

NANTES

Loire Valley

Cher

Loire

Chalonnais

Maconnais

Saône

Beaujolais

LYON

ITALY

Medoc

Blayais

Pomerol

St. Emilion

Dordogne

BORDEAUX

Entre Deux Mers

Rhône

Northern Rhône

Graves

Sauternes

Garonne

Southern Rhône

AVIGNON

Armagnac

TOULOUSE

Languedoc

MARSEILLE

Roussillon

SPAIN

The 1840s Château Longueville-Lalande in
the Médoc

In 1663, Samuel Pepys, the English diarist, penned the best-known tasting note of all time when he wrote: "Drank a sort of French wine called Ho Bryan that hath a good and most particular taste that I never met with." The wine was Haut-Brion, the first claret ever to be sold under the name of the château where the grapes were grown. The estate's owner, Arnaud de Pontac, a Bordeaux wine merchant and grandee, called the wine his First Growth. The English loved it, so he sent his son to open London's first restaurant, Pontacks Head, just beside the Old Bailey; dinner *à deux* with a bottle of Haut-Brion could cost two guineas in 1666, or $750 in today's money.

Having seen de Pontac's success, the great landowners in the Medoc started to plant vines, and the first records of vineyards at Latour, Lafite, and Margaux appear at about this time. In the eighteenth century, more famous wine estates were founded both in the Médoc and on the right bank of the Gironde in Fronsac, St.-Emilion, and Pomerol. Their names read like a roll call of red wine honor: Pichon-Longueville and Beychevelle, Leoville and Rausan, Figeac, Ausone, Magdelaine, and Trotanoy. The age of the single-vineyard château claret had arrived.

A new breed of merchants, often immigrants from northern Europe, emerged in Bordeaux as a link between the château

The old town and vineyards of St. Emilion.

proprietors and their customers in England, who comprised both landed aristocracy and the new political and industrial middle class. These powerful merchants, the *Chartronnais*, effectively controlled the wine market for well over 200 years until the late 1980s; but at the eve of the twenty-first century, with increased competition from wine producers around the world, the whip hand is with consumers who now have so many alternatives to fine Bordeaux on their shopping list.

ACROSS THE PYRENEES

Spain is the sleeping giant of wine, with more land under vine than any other country in the world. Yet, owing to the cruelly dry climate of the vast central plain of Castille and the ban on irrigation, the amount of wine she produces is relatively small compared with France and Italy. The enlightened Islamic rule of southern Spain, under whose aegis wine was appreciated, ended with the rout of the Moors at Granada in 1494. The date should ring a bell, as that year Christopher Columbus landed in the West Indies, opening Spanish colonization in Latin America.

Vineyards belonging to the Marques de Griñon, one of Spain's foremost wine-making families.

Spain

Apart from sherry and the sweet white of Malaga, there was very little wine worth exporting from the rest of Spain until the late nineteenth century. Phylloxcra, the aphid that feeds on the vine causing it to die, devastated the vineyards of France in the 1880s. Yet France's misfortune was an opportunity for Rioja, just across the Pyrenees, as French emigrants flooded into the region bringing their wine expertise and the wooden *barrique* with them. The great Riojan *bodegas* of Marques de Murrieta and Lopez de Heredia were founded at this time and were soon producing magnificent red wines that then, as now, were among the finest in the world.

The first half of the twentieth century was a time of suffering and deprivation in Spain, especially during the Spanish civil war (1936–39). The good times returned in the 1960s with the export Rioja boom to Britain. After the death of General Franco in 1975, a prosperous middle class interested in better wine emerged, and increasingly impressive reds below the price ceiling of $10 a bottle are now made across Spain, especially in Navarra, Penedes, Ribeiro del Duero, and Leon; Valdepenas, on the great plain of La Mancha, can be the best-value red wine of all.

THE ITALIAN PARADOX

Italy is a paradox, for this is a country with several thousand years' tradition of wine, a country whose Roman armies brought the vine to most parts of western Europe, a country where wine really is a part of daily living. Yet until very recently, Italy has also been the most backward country in the age of modern wine. Up to the 1970s, with the exception of Tuscany and Piedmont, very few of its better wines were exported; what went abroad were vast quantities of bulk wine–*trattoria* throat tormentors–to slake the thirst of the big Italian communities, chiefly in the United States.

The happier aspect of the paradox is that Italy is potentially a paradise for winemaking, with over 100 important indigenous grape varieties offering a wholly original range of taste sensations. And although respect for tradition is still strong, winemaking has improved immeasurably since the mid-1960s, thanks to a wave of talented and open-minded producers. Nowhere is this more evident than in Piedmont, Italy's Pauillac. If your memory of Barolo is a great red tannic monster of a wine, a delicate and refined version from the likes of Aldo Vayra or Domenico Clerico can be a revelation. In Tuscany, the tarnished image of wicker-flasked Chianti is history as winemakers have excluded the traditional (and acidic) Trebbiano grape from their red wine blends, concentrating instead on higher proportions of Sangiovese that are aged in newer, smaller barrels *à la Bordelaise*. And in the heel of the Italian boot, the bone-setting southern reds of Puglia, once essentially used to bolster northern red blends, are seeing a renaissance in excellent bottlings of the richly flavored Negro Amano grape.

Italy

SWITZERLAND

AUSTRIA

FRANCE

Valle D'Aosta

Trentino Alto-Adige

Friuli-Venezia-Giulia

Lombardy

Veneto

VENICE

Piedmont

Liguria

Emilia-Romagna

Marches

Tuscany

Umbria

Abruzzi

ROME

Lazio

Molise

Campania

Puglia

Basilicata

SARDINIA

Calabria

SICILY

The vineyards at San Guido Sassicaia in Tuscany,
Italy.

THE NEW WORLD BECKONS

Most accounts begin the American wine story with the arrival of
the Franciscan priest, Father Junipero Cerro, in southern California
in 1769 to found Mission San Diego, the first of a series of Catholic
missions that would eventually reach Sonoma, north of San
Francisco, in the next 50 years. The friars made wine, probably
from the Criolla grape, a European variety, from the start. But wine
had been produced in North America long before the Franciscans
came. According to Leon D. Adams, the American wine historian,
French Huguenots were successful winemakers in sixteenth-century
Florida; so were the early Jamestown colonists of Virginia in 1609.
Earlier still, Cortez, governor of Mexico, planted vines at El Paso
in what is now Texas.

California's wine story is a roller coaster of ups and downs. The
vineyards proliferated in the years following the Gold Rush of
1849, but the first really active trading period was at the end of the
nineteenth century; entrepreneurs made large wine fortunes and
lost them rapidly. Then came the hammer blow of Prohibition; in
1919 the whole of the U.S. went "dry" (officially, at least). When
Prohibition ended in 1933, the market was flooded with dessert

Celebrating the end of Prohibition in
New York City, 1933.

California

raisin grapes and it was not until 1968 that consumption of table wines exceeded that of dessert wines.

A critical factor in the success of California's fine wines is the use of grape varietal names such as Cabernet Sauvignon and Zinfandel since the 1970s. At the end of the twentieth century, California red wines can hold their own with the best in the world. The Cabernets regularly outshine fine clarets in blind tastings, and a small band of producers in Carneros and Santa Barbara are making Pinot Noir as good as any outside the Côte d'Or and better than much within it. California wine has come of age.

New vineyards in Los Carneros in Sonoma.

DOWN UNDER

Most wine lovers have little idea of the vast distances involved in moving from one Australian wine region to another; the journey from Western Australia's torrid Swan River to Victoria's cool Yarra Valley is as far as the voyage from Spain to Norway. So it is not surprising that Australia is, in Hugh Johnson's phrase, the France of the southern hemisphere, with the potential to make fine wines in every conceivable style. Yet the recurring theme in the Australian wine story is one of untapped potential, reflecting a lack of demand for the well-balanced refined wines that her vineyards had been able to provide from early days.

By 1850, commercially viable vineyards were producing wine grapes in every Australian state apart from Queensland and the Northern Territory. At the end of the nineteenth century the wine

Australia

Vineyards in the Barossa Valley, South Australia.

map was as extended as it is today. The period 1900–1950 was a dark time for Australian red winemakers, the vineyards shrank with the increasing consumption of fortified wine, and only a few determined companies such as McWilliams and Hardy continued to make fine wine but in tiny quantities.

Revival came, ironically, in 1953 with the ending of beer rationing. The same year, Max Schubert at Penfolds produced his first official vintage of Grange Hermitage, now revered as Australia's most famous red wine. He did so in the teeth of opposition from his bosses who decreed that a pure Shiraz (Syrah) wine would never sell.

Nearly half a century later, cool climate viticulture has made a spectacular comeback. The fog-shrouded Coonawarra district in South Australia is currently producing the continent's most sumptuous red wines, predominantly from Cabernet in a climate far cooler than either St.-Emilion or Napa Valley but with a spice-and-chocolate richness that could only be Australian.

NEW ZEALAND

Across the Tasman sea, New Zealand is better known for sheep rearing than for vine tending. In fact, vineyards were first planted in the North Island as early as 1820, though it took another 150 years for New Zealanders to appreciate that their cool climate was ideal for the growing of classic grape varieties. The lush tropical fruit flavors of Marlborough Sauvignon Blanc were all the rage in London restaurants in the 1990s. But my feeling is that New Zealand Pinot Noir, especially from the limestone soils of North Canterbury, may have the best potential of all to produce world-class red wine with finesse to rival middle-rank Burgundy.

New Zealand

GOOD HOPE FOR THE CAPE

The story of the vine in South Africa begins in 1656 with the planting of the first cuttings at the foot of Table Mountain by Jan Van Riebeeck, Governor of the Cape Colony. But it was refugee French Huguenots, arriving 30 years later, who really gave an impetus to

Painting from 1849 of the Paarl Valley in the Cape Province.

Laborie, the headquarters of KWV, the powerful
wine cooperative in South Africa.

serious winemaking. Their descendants, such as the Malans and the Jouberts, are still making wine around Paarl and Stellenbosch.

The main feature of early twentieth-century viticulture in South Africa was a serious glut of wine. The powerful cooperative system founded in 1918 by the KWV to protect the growers continues to this day. The original aims of the Kooperatieve Wijnbouwers Vereniging (KWV) to suppress overproduction were admirable, but the restraints on the planting of new vineyards have stultified progress until recently. Happily, the number of private wine estates has increased in the 1990s. The quality of the new-wave red wines is mixed owing to an odd variant of Cabernet grown in the grape. Yet in the best hands, a Shiraz from a top estate like Fairview of Paarl or a Pinot Noir from Hamilton Russell down in Hermanus at the southern tip of Africa are wines of world class to be drunk in the grandest company.

South Africa

THE QUALITY OF WINE

In the precise, critical world of Robert Parker and 100-point rating systems, it is easy to forget just how simple a drink wine can be; at the most basic level it's little more than spoiled grape juice where the sugars have been converted into alcohol. Since the arrival of the bottle and cork in the seventeenth century, though, vintners have sought to make finer and more complex wine for longer keeping. Vine growing and winemaking have long been expert tasks requiring meticulous attention to detail and acute powers of observation. Modern wine science (oenology) has further raised quality to such a technically correct level that a downright poor wine is seldom found on a retail shelf or restaurant wine list.

In order to understand what makes great wine, you have to go back to basics and consider the central idea of classic viticulture: *Terroir*. This French word, difficult to translate succinctly and shrouded in quasi-religious mystique, is a catchall term used to describe the complex interplay of natural factors–"Climate, Rock, and Soil" in Anthony Hanson's phrase–that shape the character of a vineyard and, by extension, the flavor of its wine.

CLIMATE

As good red wine in particular depends on favorable weather conditions to ripen the grapes, let's look first at climate. Some of the most subtle red wines are made in cool-climate areas where the balance between ripeness and acidity in the grapes is on a knife edge. In such conditions, the temperature of the soil and its capacity to hold the heat of the sun is crucial; the roots of the vine will grow better in warm soil and in some areas–Chinon in France's Loire Valley or Irancy in northern Burgundy are examples–this is just as important as the right type of minerals in that soil.

Academics love to classify vineyards into neat climatic zones, but this is no easy task. It involves much more than recording sunshine, cloud cover, wind, and rainfall. Factors like mountains can complicate matters, since a rise in altitude of 330 feet will reduce the average temperature by 9°F. Differences caused by such factors are best looked at in terms of the macro-, meso-, and microclimate.

The macroclimate is the climate of quite a large area, and if the terrain is diverse, information about the macroclimate will lack precision. Much more useful information can be gained by looking at the mesoclimate, which is the climate of a much smaller area, say, a particular vineyard with similar contours and elevation. The microclimate is the climate of an even smaller area, a parcel of vines, say, or the minute climatic differences affecting a grape that is, say, close to the ground compared with ones that are higher up on the same vine!

There are, of course, minimum temperatures below which the vine will not grow or develop. These vary according to grape variety–54°F for Cabernet Sauvignon but 50°F for Pinot Noir, for

SUN-HOURS IN THE WORLD'S VINEYARDS

*P*rofessor Winkler of Davis, the wine school of the University of California, devised a degree-day system that divides the vineyards of the world climatically into five regions according to the number of sun-hours recorded, 1 being the coldest and 5 the hottest. The system works well when applied to California, the region Winkler knew best. It is less accurate in a world context, not being geared to take account of variations in terrain, daylight hours, and the changing dates for harvesting the grapes in adverse or atypical vintages. Nonetheless, the following parallels and comparisons are food for thought:

REGION 1 Russian River and Santa Cruz Mountains, California; Willamette Valley, Oregon; Burgundy; Bordeaux; Neuselersee, Austria; Canterbury, New Zealand.

REGION 2 Maipo, Chile; Rutherford, California; Washington State.

REGION 3 Béziers, France, Calistoga, California.

REGION 4 Paarl & Stellenbosch, South Africa; Marches, Italy.

REGION 5 Central Valley, California; Sicily; Tunisia; Crete; Swan River, Western Australia.

example. The total number of hours during the growing season when the temperature rises above this minimum is called the heat summation. Adding up the heat summation of a region gives a good idea of its potential for fine winemaking and provides some riveting comparisons of vineyards worldwide, but with the crucial caveat that soil affects the equation differently in Europe and the New World (see box on opposite page).

SOIL

There has long been a lively debate between winemakers in Europe and the New World about the importance of soil. Jacques, a *vigneron* in Burgundy, will point to the minerals in the soil as the key to the structure and staying power of his Morey St. Denis; whereas Jim, a winegrower in Western Australia, will emphasize the dry heat of the vineyard and the nearness of the southern ocean to explain the rich spiciness and green-leaf freshness of his Margaret River Pinot Noir. Both Jacques and Jim are right *in their own sphere.* As Olivier Humbrecht, a widely traveled French viti-

Stony white soil in Languedoc-Minervois, France.

Gravel soil of Graves, France.

cultural scholar, puts it: "this difference of approach reflects different natural conditions in vineyards around the world. In France, for example, as much as half the rainfall occurs during the growing season but it is usually spread evenly throughout the season. In Australia, by contrast, rainfall during the all-important spring and summer months is often inadequate to nourish the vine, leading to a lack of moisture, producing grapes that are low in acids."

The difference of approach can be exaggerated, however, for in the 1990s growers from Australia and California travel regularly to France to make the wine at vintage time and they know as well as the French that soil really does matter. "Wine begins in the vineyard" has become a marketing cliché of our time, but it is a neat way of saying that it is essential to grow the right sort of grape in the right sort of soil.

Humbrecht reminds us that all soil is a mixture of minerals and organic matter and the particles that form soil are graded into different sizes: the largest are the stones and small gravel; fine sand is smaller, silt is composed of particles that are smaller still, and clay has the smallest particles of all. Anthony Hanson, in his seminal book *Burgundy* (Second Edition 1995), drawing on the researches of R. Gadille, writes that "the proportion of pebbles and small stones influence the drainage; that of fine clay particles, the fertility … the proportion of clay particles is capital, for they retain water and form the soil solution in which the roots of the vine develop and draw nourishment."

In all these cases, the grape variety should suit the soil. Cabernet Sauvignon ripens with difficulty in Touraine, but does so splendidly in Bordeaux and in the Frankland district of Australia's Great Southern, where there are plenty of stones and enough (but not too much) sunshine. Pinot Noir likes slightly richer soils like limestone that retain more water and are a little cooler, as in the Côte d'Or or the Canterbury district of South Island, New Zealand. The Barolo zone of Piedmont is a good example of the effect of soil on the quality of red wine. The soil here is very rich clay; the climate is warm and sunny and the Nebbiolo an early-ripening grape. Despite being made in a Mediterranean country, the resulting wine is well-balanced with good acidity owing to the high altitude of the vine-yard and the coolness of the clay soil–a textbook case of a beneficial juggling of grape variety, soil, and climate to produce a complete wine.

Red soil of Coonawarra at Rouge Homme,
South Australia.

THE VINE

It is reckoned that there are over 2,000 varieties of *Vitis vinifera*, the winemaker's vine, though about 100 of these are currently viable. For all practical purposes, the truly great red wines of the world are made from a handful of noble grape varieties. The outstanding ones are Cabernet Sauvignon, Syrah (Shiraz), and Pinot Noir, all internationally successful. Cabernet Franc, Merlot, Grenache, Mourvedre, Nebbiolo, Sangiovese, and Tempranillo are also stylish players in the quality stakes, but they often show best in their home countries or localities of origin (see Grape Varieties p. 40).

The conditions of vine-tending have a decisive impact on the quality of wine. The vine's productiveness can be increased greatly by the use of fertilizers, the choice of rootstocks and clones, and the method of pruning. But you cannot make great red wine in particular if the yields of grape juice are excessively high. The French wine authorities are altogether too relaxed about the safe

Harvesting by hand at Châteauneuf-du-Pape in the Rhône, France.

upper limits for yields in fine winemaking; the levels of production allowed in famous red Bordeaux wines can be twice as high as those of a top Cabernet Sauvignon from Santa Cruz, California or Coonawarra, Australia.

The annual biological cycle of the vine is broadly similar around the world, with less variation than you might think. In a northerly Bordeaux village like St. Estèphe, where the predominant grape is Cabernet Sauvignon, there is reckoned to be a 100-day period between the flowering of the vine and the harvest. In a hot southern hemisphere district such as the Upper Hunter Valley in New South Wales, the Cabernet's cycle may be reduced to 85 or 86 days, but not fewer. The main difference is that in northern regions, in a cold year, the grape may not be fully ripe. Conversely, in hot southern regions the problem is a lack of acidity. The Hunter Valley Cabernet Sauvignon may have just as great an imbalance as the St. Estèphe, but it is an entirely opposite one.

Another variable that can affect the quality of red wine is the chosen method of picking the grapes. With accountants breathing down their necks, winegrowers worldwide are using mechanical harvesters increasingly; the labor cost savings of a machine are obvious and, of course, it does the job far more quickly. Michel Laroche, the distinguished Chablis producer who also makes excellent red wine in the Languedoc, puts the pros and cons neatly: "There is nothing inherently wrong with a harvesting machine when the crop is healthy, but when there is a problem with rot and it is necessary to sort the grapes the machine is the wrong tool; it cannot make the necessary selection."

Mechanical harvesting in Languedoc, France.

MAKING RED WINE

In the majority of cases around the world, the grapes are first of all destalked, then crushed, and everything–pulp, pips, and skins– goes into a fermenting tank or vat after a light dosing of sulphur dioxide to prevent any biological contamination. Some winemakers in Burgundy still like to add stalks because they maintain that the stems give structure to the wine. In the tank, alcoholic fermentation is unleashed at the same time as the maceration of the grape skins and pips in the juice and lasts from five to seven days; the maceration (a process quite like a marinade in cooking) essentially gives the wine its color and staying power.

THE WINE-MAKING PROCESS

1 Grape harvest

2 Destalking the grapes

3 Crushing the grapes

4 First fermentation/maceration:
4–7 days/2–3 weeks

5 Drawing off free-run wine (*vin de goutte*)
from the fermenting tank

6 Pressing the "cake" (*marc*) to make
vin de presse, more tannic press wine

7 Careful blending of free-run wine
and press wine

8 Malolactic fermentation (conversion of
malic into lactic acid) to soften the wine

9 Clarifying the wine (sedimentation,
racking, and fining)

10 Aging the wine (in cask/*barrique* from
6 months to 2 years)

11 Bottling the wine (at 2 to 6 months for
early drinking; after 2 years for "keepers")

Sorting the grapes before crushing at Domaine de la
Romanée-Conti.

By comparison with white wine, the room for maneuver in red winemaking is considerable. In vineyards like Hermitage in the northern Rhône, the macerating period can be as long as three weeks, a treatment that gives a massive tannic structure to the finished wine. In contrast, at Henschke's great Hill of Grace vineyard in the Barossa, the same Syrah (Shiraz) grape as that used in Hermitage is only macerated in the fermenting juice for seven or eight days because this estate wants to keep the soft (as opposed to harsh) tannins in the wine; the 120-year-old vines from which it is made also have a lot to do with its glorious silken flavor.

Pressing grapes at Miguel Torres in Chile.

Fermenting grapes in an open vat at
Hunter Valley, Australia.

In Burgundy, where the natural color of Pinot Noir is a delicate
vermilion rather than a robust purple red, the *chapeau*, or cap, of
solid matter in the fermenting must is punched down two or three
times a day in order to gently extract sufficient color and tannin.
Many Burgundians still perform this task by getting half-naked into
the vat and submerging the cap with their feet, sometimes risking
their lives amid the toxic fumes of fermentation. Nowadays,
though, at the wealthier *domaines* the task is usually done by a
pneumatic machine.

Then there is the method of Guy Accad, the Burgundy
oenologist who, since the mid-1970s, has revitalized the red winemaking of several previously lackluster *domaines* on the Cote d'Or.
Accad advocates cold-soaking of the grape skins in their own juice
for two or three days prior to fermentation. The result is red wines
of deep color, which certainly makes them more saleable. The
aromas of wines made the Accad way, however, can be unsubtle
and not everyone's idea of fine red Burgundy.

Great red wine for long-keeping usually spends about 18 months
to two years maturing in fairly new oak barrels before bottling.
The use of barrels is intended less to give a woody taste, more to
impart a very slow oxidation which, together with the spice and
tannin from the oak staves, adds a touch of luxuriant complexity

to the wine. The amount of brand-new oak used should vary according to the grape variety and the relative power or delicacy of the wine and the vintage. Fine-grained and well-seasoned oak from the Troncais, Allier, and Vosges forests of France is in demand the world over, barrel-making having become big business against since the middle 1980s. New oak in winemaking is like pepper and salt in cooking: a little enhances a dish, a lot can be disastrous.

All these methods, of course, produce wines rich in tannins so they cannot be drunk immediately. A quicker winemaking method called carbonic maceration is used for red wines such as Beaujolais and Côtes du Rhône, intended to be drunk within a few months of the harvest. Here the fermentation and maceration is conducted with *whole uncrushed grapes*. The weight of the upper grapes causes the lower ones in the tank to split, setting off a normal fermentation and an attendant release of carbon dioxide, thus protecting the upper grapes from contact with air. The wines show good color and fruit but very little tannin.

Red wines for early drinking are bottled from two to six months after the harvest, whereas barrel-aged, more structured wines will wait from 18 months to two years before leaving the cask. I can never be really sure of a red wine's potential until it has been in bottle for at least a year, but no doubt other critics will disagree. *Vive la différence*!

Aging the wines in barrels
at Domaine de la Romanée-Conti.

GRAPE VARIETIES

The soil may frequently shape the structure and staying power of a fine red wine; the grape variety always determines its style and primary fruit flavors. You might think that wine should smell and taste of grapes, but, oddly enough, only scented white varieties like Muscat are really grapey; more often the flavor of grape varieties resembles that of other fruits and even vegetables, herbs, and spices. Of the top red varieties, Cabernet Sauvignon does recall black-currants, Pinot Noir red fruits like strawberries and cherries, Syrah mulberries and fresh-ground black pepper.

CABERNET SAUVIGNON

Cabernet Sauvignon is the king of noble red wine varieties and the most widely planted in the world. Its small, thick-skinned grapes ripen late and produce very deep-colored wines, often fiercely tannic when young but with an exceptional potential for aging. The Medoc and Graves districts of Bordeaux are the classic heartland of Cabernet Sauvignon. The first-growth châteaux of Latour and

Cabernet Sauvignon grapes in Mendoza, Argentina.

Mouton-Rothschild in particular have a high proportion of this variety in their grape mix; both these clarets in great years can easily live for 50 years. Yet Cabernet Sauvignon's flavor is so assertive that it often works better when classically mixed with the softer-tasting Merlot in roughly equal parts (the case with most red Bordeaux) or unconventionally with Shiraz (has been very successful in Australia).

The near-100 percent Cabernet Sauvignons produced in California in the 1970s were fearsome, heady wines, but in recent years Californian winemakers have made huge strides in taming the grape with a judicious addition of Merlot. Chile is currently making the purest expression of blackcurrant-like fruit from Cabernet Sauvignon, while Australia runs a gamut of different Cabernet styles but with a consistent softness of tannins that is very drinker-friendly.

PINOT NOIR

Pinot Noir is the queen of great red wine varieties. Delicate yet intense in flavor, mouthwateringly fruity but surprisingly complex, Pinot can make the most exciting red wine in the world, especially if grown on the limestone soil of Burgundy's Côte d'Or. But that's not the whole story, for it is a notoriously difficult variety to grow and vinify. The grapes, though early maturing, are fragile, thin-skinned, and prone to rot. They tend to thrive in a moderate climate, warm enough to ripen the fruit and ease their naturally high acidity, but also sufficiently cool to protect them against too much sunburn, high resulting alcohol, and a loss of their wonderful strawberry/cherry aromas. These problems go some way to explaining why, in Burgundy's often treacherous climate, the wines can be thin and vegetal in an off-year but sublime in a great vintage; and also why, when planted in an inappropriately hot place outside northern Burgundy, they often taste jammy and unbalanced.

However, this qualitative division between classic red Burgundy and other Pinot Noirs can be grossly exaggerated. In the cooler areas of Carneros and Santa Barbara, California, Oregon's Willamette Valley, South Africa's Walker Bay, or Australia's Yarra, vintners are making ripe yet elegant Pinots Noirs that are giving all but the best Burgundy estates some sleepless nights. For the future, the cool-climate Pinots of Martinborough and Canterbury in New Zealand may be the stars of tomorrow. Great Pinot Noir depends crucially on low yields and the imagination and flair of the wine-maker–the best names are to be found in the directory.

Syrah (Shiraz)

Syrah (Shiraz) is the crown prince of the red royal family, more powerful and ageworthy than Cabernet Sauvignon, as silken textured and gamey as great Pinot Noir when fully mature. This generalization holds true in the northern Rhône Valley, Syrah's ancestral home, where majestic red wines such as Hermitage, Côte Rôtie, and Cornas, virile and muscular, live long, distinguished lives. In the southern Rhône, especially at Châteauneuf-du-Pape, it adds structure and class to the predominant Grenache in a classic grape mix.

Syrah is a late-ripening, dark-colored grape that works best in warm soils like granite, but when overcropped it loses that intensity

Syrah (Shiraz) grapes in Languedoc-St. Chinian, France.

of mulberry fruit and black-pepper spice that is its major attraction. Sadly, that has been the case in Australia where Shiraz, Syrah's name down under, is still produced in far too great a quantity by winemakers who regard it as a workhorse grape. Yet Shiraz can still be the greatest of all Australian reds in the hands of the best producers such as Grange Hermitage and Henschke in the Barossa or Château Tahbilk in Victoria's Goulburn valley–low yields and old vines are their quality factor. Syrah is intense and Rhône-like in the Swiss region of Valais, and spicily succulent when handled by the best growers of Paarl and Stellenbosch in the Cape.

CABERNET FRANC

Cabernet Franc is a French grape variety traditionally grown in the cooler soils of Bordeaux's right bank, especially St.-Emilion and Pomerol. Lighter and faster maturing than Cabernet Sauvignon but with an aromatic fruitiness akin to raspberries, a little Cabernet Franc adds charm to a classic Bordeaux-style blend around the world. But just how good it can be when it accounts for 57 percent of the grape mix is shown in the magnificent wine of Château Cheval Blanc, the leading estate of St.-Emilion. Pure Cabernet Franc in the vineyards of Chinon and Bourgueil on the Loire can produce some of France's most pleasurable red wine, delicious when served young and slightly chilled with new season lamb, or complex when decanted at 10 years of age as a partner to roasted game birds.

MERLOT

Merlot is easily the most popular red grape variety in Bordeaux, planted in more vineyards than the two Cabernets put together. No surprise, for it is an early-ripening, fleshy, and prolific grape that produces large amounts of lush, velvety wine. It grows well in cooler districts, reaching its apogee in the densely rich and superb wines of Pomerol, notably Château Petrus. Its one drawback is that it hates heavy rainfall and is prone to rot. In the hotter vineyards of Languedoc-Roussillon, Merlot has been the most successful of the "improving grapes" introduced there since the mid-1980s, with a dramatically beneficial effect on quality. On the west coast of the

Merlot grapes at Chateau Gazin
in Pomerol, France.

U.S., Merlot's absence of harsh tannins has made it a cult wine for the beautiful people. The meticulously made Merlots of Shafer in Stag's Leap and Matanzas Creek in Sonoma are a delight.

GRENACHE

Grenache is the second most important grape variety in volume on the globe. Planted all over Spain (its reputed origin) and southern France, black Grenache or Garnacha adds spice and weight to the more refined Tempranillo in a red Rioja and is the powerful motor that drives great Châteauneuf-du-Pape and Gigondas. Quite unfazed by torrid heat, it regularly reaches 14 degrees natural alcohol in red wines that are redolent of juicy black plums tinged with Provençal herbs. When overcropped, they can be heavy and coarse, but when yields are kept low (for example at Château Rayas and Domaine St.-Gayan in the Rhône) the results can be spectacular and heartwarming. Black Grenache is increasingly used to great effect by red winemakers in Australia, such as Tim Gramp in McClaren Vale, and Catalan producers at Priorato in the hills behind Penedes. Farther up the Catalan coast into France, extraordinary black Grenache dessert wines are made in Banyuls–the best match for chocolate there is.

Grenache grapes growing in sandy soil, Languedoc-Corbieres, France.

MOURVÈDRE

Mourvèdre was the main vine of Provence until phylloxera, and though Grenache and Cinsault are now more important varieties, the small, thick-skinned Mourvèdre grape still provides the backbone and character of Bandol, Provence's greatest red wine, from vertiginous vineyards above the coast near Toulon. Mourvèdre wine shows intense blackberry fruit and strong tannins, but it does need a warm summer close to the sea to ripen fully. Bandol is thus its natural home. The grape is also used successfully to bolster a Châteauneuf-du-Pape blend and is now fashionable elsewhere in the Midi and also in California, where it is called Mataro; Ridge Vineyards in the Santa Cruz mountains makes an excellent example packed with black fruit flavors. Monastrell is the name of Mourvèdre in Spain; there it is a workhorse grape producing heady, rather volatile wine that is anything but fine.

TEMPRANILLO

Tempranillo is the aristocratic grape vine of Spain. It produces relatively early-ripening, thick-skinned grapes and deep-colored, well-structured red wines that are not too high in alcohol. So it is an ideal grape for the high altitude vineyards of Rioja Alta and

Tempranillo grapes in Rioja Alavesa, Spain.

Alavesa, accounting for 70 percent of plantings and the best fruit in the region. It blends well with Garnacha in Rioja Baja and Navarra, and is the dominant grape of the increasingly impressive reds of Ribeiro del Duero in Castille. Over the border into Portugal, Tempranillo changes its name to Tinto Rorez, one of the principal Port grapes of the Douro.

NEBBIOLO

Nebbiolo is unquestionably one of the greatest grapes, producing superlative, long-lived red wines, but it is peculiarly sensitive to site and soil and, until recently, was not seen outside northeast Italy and Piedmont in particular. The name derives from the Italian *nebbia*, or fog which shrouds the hillsides of Barolo and Barbaresco in autumn, slowing the growing season. Nebbiolo is often not harvested before mid-October and produces formidably tough wine full of acids and tannins that takes some years in bottle to soften. The wait is worth it, for a great Barolo or Barbaresco is a fascinating amalgam of flavors merging the scent of roses with a tarlike, powerful vinosity. There is a trend toward more approachable Piemontese Nebbiolo wines, which are now aged for less time in old wood barrels without any lessening of quality.

Nebbiolo grapes in Barolo, Italy.

The grape is also grown in Brescia as an ingredient in Franciacorta, and in the Val d'Aosta. A clutch of Californian growers are trying their hand with it, but as yet without dramatic results.

SANGIOVESE

Sangiovese is the ubiquitous red variety of central Italy, and the quality of the wines varies considerably. Like Pinot Noir, it mutates easily, and there are many different clones and variants divided loosely into Sangiovese Grosso and Sangiovese Piccollo. The best wines are made from the Grosso in Tuscany, exemplified in its pure, unblended form by the great slow-maturing reds of Brunello di Montalcino and the more approachable, underrated Morellino di Scansano. Sangiovese is the heartbeat of Chianti, dominating the grape mix with Canaiolo, a junior, more pliant partner. Sangiovese is a late-ripening grape that likes the limestone soils of the Chianti Classico zone between Florence and Siena; high in acidity and tannins, with an elegant, clear ruby color, it usually needs several years in bottle to reveal its characteristic aroma of irises and flavor of cherries and plums. Balance and a lingering persistence on the palate make it a red of real class. Sangiovese at its best is like good Pinot Noir, elegance rather than power its main attraction. The grape is grown successfully by Italian descendants in Argentina, and the appeal of all things Italian has triggered some promising Sangiovese wines blended with Cabernet in Napa Valley and the central coast of California.

THE COLOR OF RED WINE

*E*ditors of specialist wine magazines tend to downplay the importance of color in the appreciation of wine, considering it to be an aspect of wine tasting not worth serious coverage. This is a big mistake: the first duty of a writer in this field is to communicate the *pleasure of wine*, and the sight of a great red wine in the glass—the black-cherry hue of a young Zinfandel or the bright vermilion of an adolescent Beaune—is lovely to contemplate. And in the clinical atmosphere of a tasting room, the visual impact of a wine tells you whether it is healthy or sick.

Our eyes should observe three things: the surface of the wine both at the center of the bowl and at the rim, its color and hue, and its texture. Most modern red wines are bright and clean-looking, so any wine that is thoroughly murky (as opposed to one with a natural sediment) is faulty. The hue of red wines changes as they age, usually deep red when young but faded at the rim when old, with a brownish tint akin to maple leaves in the fall. The texture of red wine is usually measured, in the jargon, by its viscosity. This is best recognized by the "legs" of the wine, those tears of oily-looking liquid that cling to the side of the glass. Though ill-defined, the "legs" point to the levels of alcohol, glycerol, and color extraction in the wine. In a red wine made from a robust grape like Cabernet Sauvignon in a hot climate, these are a good sign; but "legs" in a subtle red Burgundy indicate a heavy hand in the winemaking and an overreliance on the sugar bags.

The following illustrated examples of red wines cover three styles, from light and delicate to strong and powerful across a representative sample of the major red grapes at various stages of maturity.

Columbia, Syrah, 1994

Domaine Drouhin, Pinot Noir, 1994

Château d'Angludet, 1994

THE APPRECIATION OF WINE

TASTING ... A FEW GROUND RULES

For anyone with a healthy sense of the ridiculous, the ritual of wine tasting is a strange and comic sight: all that peering, sniffing, gurgling, and spitting can cause the observer at best to suppress a giggle or at worst be thoroughly intimidated by the whole show. Don't be put off by the idea of "Tasting," for the difference between drinking for pleasure and tasting is simply a matter of paying greater attention. Tasting procedure is a sequence of ordered, rational steps that will hugely increase your appreciation of wine.

Start your appraisal with the eyes, as the visual impression of the wine is an important signpost to its state of health, likely character, and stage of maturity. So remove the cork gently without shaking the bottle, and pour a little red wine into a clear tulip-shaped glass to a level roughly 2 inches above the stem. Now hold the glass by the stem or foot and tilt it at an angle of 45 degrees against a white background–a pristine tablecloth or a piece of paper are ideal–and study the wine's general appearance and color (see Color of Red Wine opposite).

SMELL AND TASTE

The nose is the most sensitive organ we use when tasting wine; in fact, the sense of smell is so tightly linked with the sense of taste that the palate often confirms the sensations experienced by the nose. Hold the glass firmly by the stem and give it a good twirl to release the aromatic compounds in the wine. Then put your nose into the glass and take several short sniffs rather than one long one, as the nose tires easily, especially if you have a number of young reds to consider. Ask yourself whether you like the wine, and if you find clean, fruity aromas or harsh, unnatural odors.

Remember that just as color often points to a grape variety and stage of maturity of the wine, so may smell. Young wines release the primary fruit aroma of the grapes from which they were made. The term "aroma" is conventionally applied to what we detect with the nose in young wines; the term "bouquet" is usually employed when the wines have matured. Regarding mature red wines, the bouquet

TASTING RED WINE

Tilt the glass at an angle of 45 degrees and examine
the color of the wine.

Twirl the wine, put your nose into the glass, and take
several short sniffs.

Take a large sip and swirl it around so that it
reaches all parts of your mouth.

can run through a gamut of secondary smells, from spicy categories like cedarwood, incense, tobacco, and tar to more animal sensations such as leather and meat, especially game.

And so to the ultimate test, the impact of the wine on the palate and its texture in the mouth. Take a large sip and, drawing air over the wine, swirl it around so that it reaches all parts of your mouth. This allows the tongue to appreciate fully the three main sensations of sweetness at the tongue's tip, acidity at the sides, and bitterness at the back. Tasting red wines is slightly more complicated than just considering sweetness and acidity as one would for white wines, for red wine is made with its skins, pips, and occasionally stalks. These give it a different mouth-feel and different sorts of flavors. Young red wines, particularly those made from the Cabernets, Syrah, or Nebbiolo, usually have high levels of tannin–that furry, dry feeling that makes them difficult to drink immediately–but it gradually diminishes as they age in bottle. Red Burgundy and other top-flight wines made from Pinot Noir are quite different; they have a succulent, silky texture and an intense lingering aftertaste when just a couple of years old. The "finish" of a red wine, that is, the length of time the flavor stays with you after you have swallowed the wine, is a surefire indication of any potentiality for greatness.

When drinking wine, the glass should be
about one third full.

STORING RED WINE

For most readers, the important point is to keep things simple. Starting a wine cellar or nest egg requires a little resourcefulness now that so many of us live in centrally heated apartments or houses without cellars. If you have bought several case lots of fine wine that you don't want to drink for years, a good independent wine merchant will store them for you in an air-conditioned warehouse for a small rent. For those who have just two or three dozen bottles, the guiding principles are:

• store the wines horizontally on their sides in as quiet and dark a spot as possible

• keep the wines well away from points of heat

• be careful to ensure that the temperature of the place of storage does not fluctuate too wildly (avoid a working kitchen, the garage, and the garden shed)

For the ambitious collector who needs more space, a good option is to buy a prefabricated "cellar" that can be installed in the home. There are two types. The electric temperature-controlled cabinet, specially designed to store wine, comes in various shapes and sizes and can be plugged in anywhere. More ambitious still is the spiral staircase. The best make is Eurocave; the unit comprises a large steel cylinder with a spiral staircase, the wine bins slotting into spaces within the body of the cylinder and between the stairs. Obviously, a large hole has to be dug to accommodate the unit; a distinguished French wine writer had one installed in the floor of his bathroom at his apartment block in Paris!

SERVING RED WINE

Red wines are usually drunk too warm. Ideally, they should be served at a slightly cooler temperature (say, 60° Fahrenheit) than the ambient norm of a well-heated apartment. Never put a bottle of good red wine on a hot stove or radiator; it will simply taste like a crudely alcoholic soup. Light, young, and fruity reds–Beaujolais, Chinon, Bardolino–can be quite delicious served slightly chilled with a summer lunch.

Young red wines with high levels of tannins and acids do benefit by being opened 30 minutes before they are served, especially if they are first poured into a jug: this has a softening effect on the wines. In the case of venerable aged wines for immediate drinking, be more cautious by letting them "breathe" for as little as five minutes in order to get rid of any bottle stink. Remember that old wine is fragile and its subtle bouquet can be easily destroyed by too much aeration, which brings us to the thorny subject of decanting. Decanters can certainly be a magnificent sight, particularly the large magnum-size ones; any fine wine retailer should stock a good range. Decanting a young red wine helps round out the rough edges, but it is only essential if the wine has a heavy sediment or deposit, vintage or crusted port being the most extreme case.

RED WINE AND HEALTH

*A*s early as 1980, the *American Journal of Medicine* published a study of the three great causes of mortality—cancers, coronary disease, and cerebral vascular accidents (strokes)—in relation to the consumption of alcohol. This study and many others since have firmly established that alcohol has a protective effect against coronary disease because it raises the rate of "good" cholesterol (known as HDL) in the bloodstream: a higher rate of HDL in the plasma causes a marked reduction in the frequency of heart attacks. Wine consumption received a further fillip in the 1990s when a Lyonnais nutritionist, Dr. Serge Renaud, found that animal-fat derived lipids ("bad" cholesterol) in the bloodstream can be reduced by the tannins in wine, particularly red wine, which is usually tannin-rich. A documentary on *Sixty Minutes* gave U.S. prime-time television coverage to Dr. Renaud's findings, which have since caused a huge increase in red wine consumption in the U.S. As the British wine writer Stuart Walton puts it: "the manufacturers of anticoagulant drugs might have something to lose if we all got the message that we would do just as well by our hearts … by taking half a bottle of red wine every day."

Personally, I never decant fine red Burgundy, fearing I may lose its subtleties of scent and flavor in the process. If you do decide to decant, stand the bottle upright for 24 hours so that the sediment settles at the bottom. Uncork the wine and pour it in a steady, slow stream into the decanter, always keeping an eye on the neck of the bottle. Once you see the first traces of any deposit passing through the neck, stop pouring. If you do the job carefully, you will be surprised by how little wine is lost. Don't bother with the murky residue–throw it away to avoid any temptation to use it in a gravy or sauce. And never use paper coffee filters or tissues, as they can make a $20 bottle of wine taste like a $3 one.

GLASSES

The general rule for fine wine glasses is that they should be simple, plain, unadorned, and tulip-shaped. The Austrian glass designer Georg Riedel has made a special study of their optimal shape, and his top-of-the-range Sommelier glasses, particularly the generously sized Bordeaux and Burgundy glasses, are ideal.

Tulip-shaped glasses are ideal for drinking. From left to right: Syrah, Burgundy, Bordeaux, and Barillo.

PART TWO

THE RED WINE
directory

THE RED WINE *directory*

CLASSICS

CASTELL'IN VILLA

Azienda Agricola Castell'in Villa,
53033 Castelnuovo Berargenga (Siena) Italy
Tel: (0577) 359074 Fax: (0577) 359222
Visitors: by appointment only

*F*rom the hills east of Siena, the wines of Castell'in Villa closely resemble their maker. Coralia Pignatelli is a hardworking widow of great charm and formidable strength of character. She was born in Greece and spent much of her early life in Switzerland, where she met and married Principe Riccardo Pignatelli della Leonessa, an Italian diplomat and member of the old Roman nobility.

Looking for a retreat from the demands of ambassadorial life, the couple bought Castell'in Villa in 1968. Their decision must have certainly been influenced by its superb views over the Tuscan countryside toward the towers of Siena.

FACT BOX

OWNER: Principessa Coralia Ghertsos Pignatelli della Leonessa

WINEMAKER: Principessa Pignatelli

SIZE OF VINEYARD: 135 acres

TOTAL ANNUAL PRODUCTION: 30,000 cases

GRAPE VARIETIES: Sangiovese, Cabernet Sauvignon (for Santa Croce)

AVERAGE AGE OF VINES: 30 years

PERCENTAGE OF NEW WOOD: Upward of 50 percent

BEST RECENT VINTAGES: 1995, 1993, 1990, 1988

BEST DISHES TO MATCH WINE: spit-roasted Easter lamb, game

OWN RESTAURANT: Yes

In the course of 30 years, Princess Pignatelli's estate has become one of the "greats" of Tuscany, her Chiantis much admired (not least by the Antinoris) for their consistent refinement allied to a structured depth of flavor–a model expression of the Sangiovese grape grown in the warmer soils of the southern part of the Classico zone. Pignatelli is particularly adept at making stylish wine in difficult years such as 1972, 1987, and 1989, and in good years (1990 and 1995 especially) her *riservas* are almost always among the best four or five wines of the vintage.

The Princess also makes the mightily impressive Santa Croce, a prestige red *vino da tavola* sourced essentially from Sangiovese and a little Cabernet Sauvignon from her ideally sited Balsastrada vineyard close to the Castello. This is one of the great red wines of the world, the acme of power and elegance. And if that was not enough, she just happens to produce one of Tuscany's best olive oils. All these delights can be savored in the vineyard's own restaurant, surrounded by silver olive trees that must remind this extraordinary woman of her beloved Greece.

TASTING NOTES

SANTA CROCE 1988

Extraordinary youthful color for a 10-year-old wine, the richest shade of shimmering ruby; superb tannic power and deep flavor in no way mitigate against its remarkable finesse. Will live and develop until at least 2115. Knocks several more highly priced grand cru St. Emilions into a cocked hat. *Ne plus ultra.* Last tasted November 1997.
Rating ★★★★★

CHÂTEAU CHEVAL BLANC

33330 St. Emilion, France
Tel: (33-5) 57 55 55 55 Fax: (33-5) 57 55 55 50
Visitors: strictly by appointment only

*L*ong regarded as one of the eight greatest growths of Bordeaux, Château Cheval Blanc in good vintages is an incomparable claret of sumptuous texture and powerful, yet delicate, flavor. The unique personality of the wine is due to the top-quality soil of its vineyard, located on the border with the Pomerol *appellation*, and to an unusual blend of grape varieties.

The soil is quite a complex mix. In different parts of the vineyard, there is

FACT BOX

OWNERS: Société Civile du Cheval Blanc (Fourcas-Laussac family)

WINEMAKER: Kees Van Leeuwen

SIZE OF VINEYARD: 90 acres

SECOND WINE: Petit Cheval

TOTAL ANNUAL PRODUCTION: 10,000 cases (*grand vin*); 3,000 cases (Petit Cheval)

GRAPE VARIETIES: Cabernet Franc 57 percent; Merlot 41 percent; Cabernet Sauvignon 1 percent; Malbec 1 percent

AVERAGE AGE OF VINES: 35 years

PERCENTAGE OF NEW WOOD: 100 percent (*grand vin*); 50 percent (Petit Cheval)

BEST RECENT VINTAGES: 1995, 1994, 1990, 1988

BEST DISHES TO MATCH WINES: medallions of roe deer, roast grouse, *filet de boeuf en croute*

LOCAL RESTAURANTS: Francis Gaulle, Plaisance, Le Tertre: all in St. Emilion

sandy soil and gravelly soil, both on clay subsoils, and there is also a deep layer of gravel in a third part. Forgive the geology lesson, but the combined characteristics of these different plots are extremely conducive to the growing of high-quality wine grapes. For example, the clay beneficially regulates water supply to the vine roots, while the gravel and sand create a warm microclimate that promotes early ripeness. And crucially, the autumn rains inherent to an Atlantic climate generally have less influence here than in other parts of Bordeaux.

To take full advantage of its unique soil, this estate has a large proportion of Cabernet Franc (57 percent), this very elegant grape variety giving Cheval Blanc its inimitable flavor and mouthfeel. As a matter of policy, the yields are kept quite low. The tannic power of Cabernet Franc blends beautifully with the soft juiciness of Merlot (41 percent). At harvest time in the vat house, the wine is left on its skins for an average of three weeks and then run off. The *grand vin* is aged in 100 percent new oak barrels for about 18 months. The second wine, Petit Cheval, ages for approximately 12 months in 50 percent new barrels. The *grand vin* is not filtered.

This detailed account of vineyard practices and

> ## TASTING NOTES
>
> ### CHATEAU CHEVAL BLANC 1995
>
> Deep, dark ruby with mauve highlights, typically sumptuous Cheval Blanc aromas, black fruits (cherry and blackcurrant). Superb ripeness and spice on entry. Huge concentration on the palate, beautiful soft tannins on finish. Spectacular, as strong on charm as on structure.
>
> Rating ★★★★★

Aging the *grand vin*.

Château Cheval Blanc in St. Emilion, Bordeaux.

winemaking at Cheval Blanc hopefully gives you some idea of the perfectionist principles that guide the management team led by Pierre Lurton and Kees Van Leeuwen. At the end of the 1990s, this is truly a First Growth in spirit as well as official status, superb wines having been made in 1995 and 1990, worthy successors to the great 1985, the greater 1982, and the legendary 1947.

CHATEAU COS D'ESTOURNEL

33180 St. Estèphe, France
Tel: (33-5) 56 73 15 30 Fax: (33-5) 56 59 72 59
Visitors: by appointment only

*C*os d'Estournel is a natural site for making great red wine. Separated from Château Lafite by a little brook that you cross as you come from Pauillac into the commune of St. Estèphe, the hill of Cos rises to a height of almost 60 feet above the Gironde Estuary. The stone and gravel slope has given the property its name, Cos (pronounced Coss, like the lettuce), meaning the "Hill of Pebbles" in the old Gascon tongue. The porousness of this soil and its perfect drainage ensure that water never accumulates on the hill, so forcing the vines to thrust their

FACT BOX

OWNERS: Société des Domaines Prats
WINEMAKER: Bruno Prats
SIZE OF VINEYARD: 162.5 acres
SECOND LABEL: Les Pagodes de Cos
TOTAL ANNUAL PRODUCTION: 30,000 cases
GRAPE VARIETIES: Cabernet Sauvignon 60 percent; Merlot 38 percent; Cabernet Franc 2 percent
AVERAGE AGE OF VINES: 40 years
PERCENTAGE OF NEW WOOD: between 40 and 80 percent
BEST RECENT VINTAGES: 1996, 1990, 1989, 1986, 1985, 1982
BEST BUY: 1994
BEST DISHES TO MATCH WINES: roast partridge, guinea fowl
LOCAL RESTAURANT: Château Cordeillan-Bages

roots deep into the subsoil to find nourishment. This slows down the flow of the vine's sap, concentrating it and giving the grapes a particular flavor.

The *grand cru* vineyard we know today was created by Louis-Gaspard d'Estournel between 1810 and 1850. A man of imagination and vision, he quickly grasped just how excellent the environment of Cos was for growing grapes and decided to purchase the whole of the hill. An obsessive bachelor, he lived and breathed the wine, traveling tirelessly across the oceans of the world to spread the good word, and even managed to build a market in India.

Louis-Gaspard noticed that his wine improved during the course of its long sea voyage, so he had some of the wine returned from the subcontinent marked "R," meaning "Returned from India." This he offered to his distinguished house guests, who nicknamed him the "Maharajah of St. Estèphe." His fame must have touched his brain, for in 1830, as a commemoration of his Asian journeys, Louis-Gaspard built a fantastical palace in oriental style to house his cellars. The pagoda of Cos is a striking landmark of the Médoc and a continuing place of pilgrimage for claret lovers. The list of famous clients of the wine since the mid-nineteenth century is long: In 1857, Friedrich Engels sent six bottles of Cos d'Estournel to Karl

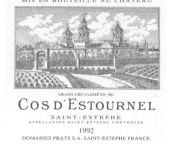

Marx with a note saying "it will do your wife good." Is this an early example of radical chic?

Since 1970 Bruno Prats, whose family owns Cos, has been responsible for the wines. The very model of a modern winemaker with degrees in agronomy and oenology, Bruno looks more like a benign physician than a *vigneron*. He has certainly taken the château to the front rank of Bordeaux properties. In his hands, technical competence always plays a supporting role to a respect for the remarkable *terroir* of his vineyard. At Cos, this is a complex matter. On the thin gravel at the top of the hill and south slopes, Cabernet Sauvignon (60 percent of the vineyard) finds its ideal soil. On the east limestone slopes Merlot (just under 40 percent) is planted. The relatively high percentage of Merlot gives the wine a supple, rounded personality, but this approachable aspect is deceptive, for Cos is at heart a strong, powerful claret with great capacity for aging. Another shaping influence on the wine is a preference for late picking, the date for harvesting being chosen parcel by parcel. The result is a finished wine of mellow tannins that tastes good throughout its very long life. Since 1982, Cos d'Estournel has been turning out a succession of magnificent wines, in my view as good as the first growths in several instances. The 1990 is an especially graceful wine, a true classic.

> ## TASTING NOTE
>
> ### CHATEAU COS D'ESTOURNEL 1990
>
> Lovely deep ruby, no sign of age; sensuous nose of ripe red fruits and a subtle touch of smoky oak; superb palate, classically structured, deeply flavored, with a velvety texture. Exceptionally long aftertaste suggests a very long life to come (good until 2020). One of the greatest 1990s.
> Rating ★★★★★

The Asian-inspired logo on some of the bottles is testament to Louis Gaspard d'Estournel's love of India.

CHATEAU DE BEAUCASTEL

84350 Courthezon, France
Tel: (33-4) 90 70 41 00 Fax: (33-4) 90 70 41 19
Visitors: by appointment

*T*his is the leading estate of Châteauneuf-du-Pape, producing superb wines that are consistently subtler, finer, and longer lived than any other in the *appellation*. Taking its name from Pierre de Beaucastel, a Huguenot landowner, the estate has been growing grapes since at least the 1830s. Currently owned and run by the perfectionist brothers, François and Jean-Pierre Perrin, the vineyard, located in the

FACT BOX

OWNERS: François and Jean-Pierre Perrin

WINEMAKER: François Perrin

SIZE OF VINEYARD: 175 acres (Châteauneuf du Pape); 87.5 acres (Côtes du Rhône)

TOTAL ANNUAL PRODUCTION: 25,000 cases (red wines)

GRAPE VARIETIES: Grenache 30 percent; Mourvedre 30 percent; Syrah 10 percent; Cinsault 5 percent; remaining 25 percent other permitted varieties, notably Counoise

AVERAGE AGE OF VINES: 50 years

PERCENTAGE OF NEW WOOD: None (for red wines)

BEST RECENT VINTAGES: 1995, 1990, 1989, 1988, 1983, 1981, 1978

BEST DISHES TO MATCH WINES: *Filet de Boeuf aux champignons, salmi de faisin*

LOCAL RESTAURANT: La Beaurivière, Mondragon

eastern part of the *appellation* toward Courtezon, extends to 175 acres planted with all 13 grape varieties permitted in the making of Châteauneuf-du-Pape. Significantly, the proportion of Grenache

grown at Beaucastel (30 percent) is well under half that of most other Châteauneuf estates because the Perrins want to produce a structured wine that is not too alcoholic.

In the vineyard, the biodynamic methods of Rudolf Steiner are followed; in particular the use of herbicides and pesticides is suppressed. As the winemaker, François practices a special technique, introduced by his father, called *vinification à chaud*. The grapes are first heated by steam to a temperature of 176°F for around one and a half minutes. The benefits are good extraction of color and the elimination of bacteria, thus removing the need to use sulfur or cultured yeasts. Vatting lasts for up to 21 days, during which time the grape skins are regularly punched down, an idea borrowed from Gérard Chave

Storing bottles of old vintages at
Château de Beaucastel.

The wine is aged in old oak for up to fourteen months.

of Mauves. François does not like new wood, preferring to age his reds in large, used oak *foudres* for six to 14 months depending on the vintage. The wines are rested for at least a year after bottling so that they reach the customer in prime condition.

Beaucastel is one of the great red wines of France, so it is hard to describe its complexities adequately. The initial aromas in the young wine suggest hedgerow fruits, but with everything held in reserve; after six or seven years the bouquets become strikingly rich, the flavors spicy and gamey. The wines age magnificently, with the 1978 and 1981 well able to provide great pleasure right into the first years of the twenty-first century. The Perrins also run a Côtes du Rhône estate, producing a wine called Coudoulet de Beaucastel with something of the same elegance and character of the *grand vin*, but quicker-maturing and, of course, considerably less expensive.

TASTING NOTES

CHATEAU DE BEAUCASTEL, CHATEAUNEUF-DU-PAPE 1994

Middle to deep Victoria plum; nose completely closed 10 minutes after drawing the cork, then six hours later, a burgeoning smell of raspberries, but still tight. Structure, elegance, Provençal herbal tones on the palate are all here, but the flavors are only half formed. Great potential. Drink from 2001. Tasted November 1997.

Rating ★★★★

DOMAINE DE CHEVALIER

33850 Leognan, France
Tel: (33-5) 56 64 16 16 Fax: (33-5) 56 64 18 18
Visitors: by appointment, weekdays only

*T*he setting gives little clue to the greatness of the wines. The Domaine de Chevalier is a charming but relatively modest single-story house, set in the middle of a pine forest to the southwest of Leognan. Only the cylindrically shaped new *cuverie* full of gleaming stainless-steel fermenters gives you some idea of the large sums invested here by the wealthy Bernard spirits family, who bought the property in 1983 from Claude Ricard.

For much of the twentieth century, Chevalier has produced small quantities of outstanding white and red wine, in either

FACT BOX

OWNER: Olivier Bernard
WINEMAKER: Thomas Streetstone and Remi Edange
SIZE OF VINEYARD: 74 acres (red wines)
TOTAL ANNUAL PRODUCTION: 7,000 cases (red wines)
GRAPE VARIETIES: Cabernet Sauvignon 65 percent; Merlot 30 percent; Cabernet Franc 5 percent
AVERAGE AGE OF VINES: 25 years
PERCENTAGE OF NEW WOOD: 50 percent
BEST RECENT VINTAGE: 1996
BEST DISHES TO MATCH WINES: roast leg of lamb, grilled meats, game
LOCAL RESTAURANT: Le St. James, Boullac

color among the best of the Graves (and now Pessac-Leognan) *appellation*. Finesse allied to structure is looked for in the red wine, which is fermented to a higher than usual temperature of 89.6°F. This is not to extract maximum tannins from the grapes, as one writer on Bordeaux has suggested, but rather to encourage the supple, velvety aspect–the *gras*–of the wine. Another originality of red wine-making at Chevalier is the continued use

of *bombage*, a procedure akin to the Burgundian *pigeage*, which,

through the use of a wooden shaft, punches down the grape skins in order to obtain a gentle extraction of color and consequently greater harmony in the finished wine. Barrel aging lasts for 14–24 months, the percentage of new oak varying from 40 to 70 percent depending on the vintage. For wine-makers at de Chevalier Thomas Stonestreet and Remi Edange, "The reds of Chevalier have those round tannins, very fine and

Olivier Bernard, Administrator at Domaine de Chevalier.

The vineyards on the de Chevalier estate.

tight, characteristic of wines of finesse and distinction; more delicate than powerful, their flavors are those of little red fruits (raspberries), licorice, and spices."

Especially fine long-lived wines were made here in 1986 and 1988. Olivier Bernard believes that the 1996, a great Cabernet year, may be the best red wine he has produced since coming here as a young man of 21 in 1983 to sit at the feet of Claude Ricard.

TASTING NOTES

DOMAINE DE CHEVALIER 1996

Deep purple ruby but elegant, not over-extracted; superb Cabernet-dominant nose, cassis, raspberries: impressive depth, definition of flavor and length; silky tannins; typical tight Chevalier structure. A real classic, drink from 2006.

Rating ★★★★★

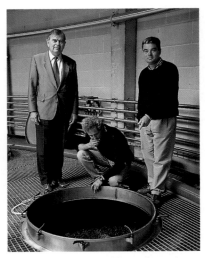

Thomas Stonestreet (*middle*), is the Enologist at de Chevalier.

DOMAINE DE LA ROMANÉE-CONTI

SC du Dom. de la Romanée-Conti,
21700 Vosne Romanée, France
Tel: (33-3) 80 61 04 57
Visitors: by appointment only

*F*or many people this very famous *domaine*, known to connoisseurs simply as DRC, is the greatest estate on the Côte d'Or, producing wines of extraordinary richness and complexity. Its 67.5 acres of vineyards in the finest sites of Vosne-Romanée and Flagey-Echezeaux, not forgetting a parcel of Le Montrachet, is the most expensive piece of real estate in Burgundy. The vineyards include, of course,

FACT BOX

OWNERS: SC du Domaine de la Romanée-Conti

WINEMAKER: Aubert de Villaine and Henry-Frederic Roche

SIZE OF VINEYARD: 67.5 acres

TOTAL ANNUAL PRODUCTION: 7,000 cases

GRAPE VARIETY: Pinot Noir (excluding Chardonnay in Le Montrachet)

AVERAGE AGE OF VINES: 47 years

PERCENTAGE OF NEW WOOD: 100 percent

BEST RECENT VINTAGES: 1995, 1993, 1990, 1988, 1985

BEST BUY: 1992

BEST DISHES TO MATCH WINES: milk-fed lamb and piglet; woodcock and grouse

LOCAL HOTEL RESTAURANT: La Côte d'Or, Saulieu

the *domaine*'s word-famous monopoles of Romanée-Conti and La Tache, but also nearly half of Richebourg, more than half of Romanée-Saint-Vivant, and over a third of Grands Echezeaux.

The prestige of these holdings is fully matched by the *domaine*'s commitment to the highest standards of vineyard tending and wine-making under the care of Aubert de Villaine, DRC's discreet driving force, and his talented co-director, Henry-Frederic Roche. The average age of the vines is impressively mature (Romanée Conti's is 47 years, that of La Tache 45 years). Pesticides and other chemical treatments are avoided.

The DRC was one of the first estates to introduce an automated conveyor to sort imperfect grapes at harvest time. The top four *grands crus* are traditionally fermented in open-topped wooden casks, while the Grands Echezeaux and Echezeaux are vinified in open-topped

> ### TASTING NOTE
>
> ### LA TACHE
> ### 1991
>
> Refracted, multitoned, rich clear-red color; latent complex aromas will become ethereal with more aging; magical balance of power and finesse, ripe tannins cloak the mouth, an exceptional La Tache from an unsung year. Needs time. Drink from 2001.
> Rating ★★★★★

Old and extremely rare bottles of Romanée-Conti.

stainless-steel tanks, the grapes being automatically punched down. All the DRC wines are aged in new oak, but great care is taken to ensure that the barrel staves have been properly matured.

Very few would now question the claim that the DRC wines are among the best of the best. Words are hopelessly inadequate to describe their magic, but they do have great finesse and intensity, allied to an extraordinary long flavor that stays with you for several minutes after you have put down your glass. Of all the wines, La Tache is my favorite, as it is for many other critics. Its haunting bouquet and refinement belies a very durable structure; truly this is the ultimate red Burgundy and as satisfying in so-called average years (1991 and 1987, for example) as in great ones (1993, 1990, 1988, 1962, 1959).

Picking grapes at Romanée-Conti.

DOMAINE DE THALABERT, CROZES-HERMITAGE

041 Paul Jaboulet Aine,
26660 La Roche de Glun, France
Tel: (33-4) 75 84 68 93 Fax: (33-4) 75 84 56 14
Visitors: 9:00AM–11:00AM and 2:00PM–5:00PM

*E*stablished in 1834, for many years the celebrated house of Paul Jaboulet Aine (PJA) enjoyed a well-earned reputation as the pre-eminent source of top-flight wines from the Rhône valley. Since the mid-1980s, however, Jaboulet's poll position has been usurped by Guigal among *negociants-proprietaires*. And Hermitage growers' wines from such stars as Gerard and Jean-Louis Chave or Bernard Faurie are now more sought after than PJA's Hermitage La Chapelle (save for its superb 1990).

Jaboulet's one ace card is its 100-acre Crozes-Hermitage Domaine de Thalabert

FACT BOX

OWNERS: Jaboulet family
WINEMAKER: Philippe Jaboulet
SIZE OF VINEYARD: 100 acres
TOTAL ANNUAL PRODUCTION:
15,000 cases
GRAPE VARIETY: Syrah
AVERAGE AGE OF VINES:
15–20 years
PERCENTAGE OF NEW WOOD:
10–35 percent
BEST RECENT VINTAGES: 1995, 1994, 1991, 1990, 1988
BEST DISHES TO MATCH WINES:
red meat and game

which, in John Livingstone-Learmonth's phrase, produces "*Grand Vin* at a tiny price." For the last 25 years, this marvelous wine, a great expression of the Syrah grape's rich fruit and spice, has been utterly dependable in powerful vintages (1983, 1988, 1990, 1995) and lighter ones (1987, 1991).

The Domaine de Thalabert is situated in the prime Crozes *lieu-dit* of Les Chassis on an old stone plain of glacial origin. Winemaking is classical; extended vatted times are followed by 12–16 months aging in oak *pièces*. The amount of new wood is restricted to a range of 10–35 percent

depending on the vintage. Generally speaking, Thalabert drinks very well after five–seven years in bottle.

The old church at Domaine de Thalabert.

TASTING NOTES

DOMAINE DE THALABERT, CROZES- HERMITAGE 1981

A fascinating bottle greatly superior to one's expectations for the *Crozes Appellation*. Deep sombre ruby with mauve highlights; durably structured for the year; slowly evolving mulberry fruitiness, a mightily impressive length of flavor underpinned by elegant tannins; beautifully made, this tastes of ripe mature wine rather than new oak—a classic northern Rhône and great value for money.

Rating ★★★★

MAISON JOSEPH DROUHIN

7 rue d'Enfer, 21200 Beaune, France
Tel: (33-3) 80 24 68 88 Fax: (33-3) 80 22 43 14
Visitors: by appointment only

*W*hen I was a green, wine-trade apprentice in Beaune at the end of the 1960s, making sense of the maze of Burgundy wasn't easy. Those were the days before the laws of *appellation contrôlée* were enforced, and all sorts of wine from the Midi and points south found their way into a bottle labeled Nuits-St.-Georges or Gevrey-Chambertin. If you wanted a benchmark of the real thing, Maison Drouhin was one of a handful of houses you could absolutely rely on. But then Robert Drouhin, the head of this family firm since 1957, has always been a man with a clear, unshakable conviction that Burgundy is

FACT BOX

OWNERS: Snowhill Farms (Japan)

WINEMAKERS: Laurence Jobard and Veronique Boss-Drouhin

TOTAL ANNUAL PRODUCTION: 100,000 cases

AVERAGE AGE OF VINES: 32 years (Clos des Monches)

GRAPE VARIETY: Pinot Noir (for reds)

PERCENTAGE OF NEW WOOD: not disclosed

BEST RECENT VINTAGES: 1996, 1995, 1993, 1990

BEST DISHES TO MATCH WINES: game, guinea fowl, baby lamb

LOCAL RESTAURANT: La Côte d'Or, Saulieu

all about outstanding wines of complete authenticity. Apart from its impressive venture of establishing Domaine Drouhin, Oregon in 1988, the firm has never traded in wines outside Burgundy.

Maison Drouhin is probably best known for its excellent white wines and owns a large vineyard of 92.5 acres in Chablis, with a sizable portion in *grand & premier crus*. But maybe the real glories here are the red wines. The monopole of Beaune Clos des Mouches is Drouhin's signature vineyard. Although nowadays it produces both white and red wine, the latter in

> ## TASTING NOTES
>
> ### BEAUNE CLOS DES MOUCHES 1995
>
> Vivid elegant ruby; aromas of fruity yet surprisingly complex Pinot Noir, essentially cherries, with a touch of spicy toasted new oak; poised minty-fresh flavors will cede to secondary gamey tastes with more bottle age. Drink from 2000.
> Rating ★★★

particular is a blue-chip Beaune in which the purity of Pinot Noir fruit, the gently expressive influence of the vineyard's *terroir*, and a finely judged use of oak combine to produce a classic red Burgundy of real class. Also, since 1960, Robert Drouhin has made every effort to develop the estate in the Côte de Nuits, which now has holdings in the greatest sites such as Chambertin, Clos-de-Bèze, Bonnes Mares, Musigny, Clos de Vougeot, and several more.

Essentially traditional methods finessed by modern techniques characterize Drouhin vineyard tending and winemaking. The firm has its own nursery of vines, grapes are picked entirely by hand, and a high proportion of wooden *barriques* are employed to vinify and age the wines, though the amount of new oak is sparing. "We are winemakers, not carpenters," say the Drouhins, with feeling.

Robert's children take an active part in the business: Frederic assists his father in the general management team; Philippe runs the estates of the Côte d'Or; Véronique (an oenologist) is the winemaker at Domaine Drouhin, Oregon; Laurent is a regional commercial director. With such a brood of enthusiasts the future at Drouhin looks bright, as long as they are left in peace to continue making authentic Burgundy by the majority Japanese shareholders in the business.

Thirteenth century cellars of the
Collegiate in Beaune.

PIERRE-JACQUES DRUET

Le Pied-Fourrier, 7 rue de la Croix Rouge,
Benais, 37140 Bourgueil, France
Tel: (33-2) 47 97 37 34 Fax: (33-2) 47 97 46 40
Visitors: anytime with advance notice

*S*tarting with nothing in 1980, Pierre-Jacques Druet has become the most respected grower in Bourgueil and the maker of the Loire's greatest red wine in less than 20 years. His father was a broker and salesman of bulk wines further up the river in Montrichard, but the young Pierre-Jacques always wanted to be a winemaker and went off to learn the basics at the Lycée Viticole in Beaune, finishing his studies at Montpellier and Bordeaux with the best marks for oenology in his class. He took various well-paid jobs in the wine business, both as a technocrat and

FACT BOX

OWNER & WINEMAKER:
Pierre-Jacques Druet

SIZE OF VINEYARD: 55 acres

TOTAL ANNUAL PRODUCTION:
8,000 cases

GRAPE VARIETY: Cabernet Franc

AVERAGE AGE OF VINES: 50 years,
some over 95 years

PERCENTAGE OF NEW WOOD:
10 percent (Troncais, steamed, not
toasted)

BEST RECENT VINTAGES: 1996, 1995,
1993, 1990, 1989

BEST DISHES TO MATCH WINES:
classic French food for red; Asiatic
cooking for rosé

LOCAL RESTAURANTS: Jean Bardet in
Tours, Jacky Dallais in Petit Pressigny

salesman, saved some money, got married, and started looking for his own vineyard. A patient and determined fellow, he rejected settling in Provence, Burgundy, and Bordeaux. By chance, on a visit to his homeland in the Loire, he came across some very old vines in the village of Benais, near Bourgueil, rushed into the village to find out who owned them and was delighted to discover that it was an old lady who wanted to lease the vines and the dilapidated winery that went with them. Pierre-Jacques signed up immediately, as he knew he could make great red wine here from the start. He won a string of gold medals with his first vintage, which did not endear him to the Benais villagers, but being kind *Touraine* folk they slowly came to like him, in part because of his great personal charm but more realistically because he was always ready to help his fellow winemakers out of a hole.

A logical man with a scientist's mind, Pierre-Jacques keeps a watchful eye on the latest technological advances and harnesses them to help his winemaking. Small, conical, stainless-steel vats with very exact temperature controls are used to ferment all the red

---

TASTING NOTES

BOURGUEIL VAUMOREAU 1990

Still deep-black purple at seven years of age, but elegant and lustrous. The aromas and bouquet a quintessence of spices like cinnamon and sandalwood layered on a base of the most ripe fruit flavors that come from very old vines. The palate defies description, being ultra-complex yet inviting with its mouth-coating tannins and vinosity. Needs to be kept until 2005 before drawing the cork, and well-cellared will live into the middle of the twenty-first century. Très grand vin. Last tasted September 1997.

Rating ★★★★★

wines. They are then aged not in small *barriques*, which might give too woody a taste, but in large 182-gallon oak tuns for 18 months to four years, depending on the weight of the wine and the part of the vineyard it comes from. Pierre-Jacques makes a lovely, delicate yet multiflavored rosé, the one wine he ferments in wood to round

out the sharp edges of acidity. He also makes a red Chinon from old vines, the Clos du Danay—impeccably made, of course, but somehow it doesn't sing for me.

The world-class wines in this cellar are the four Bourgueils. Les Cents Boisselles with bold primary Cabernet Franc flavors

is ready soonest. The Beauvais is a complete wine with a fine balance of vinosity and oak, enlivened with the wild blackberry

fruit flavors of the best Bourgueil. Grand Mont is altogether more concentrated and tannic. The spectacular Vaumoreau, a monumental wine made from 50- to 100-year old vines, is black as Egypt's night and the very essence of the complex inter-play of spiced fruit flavors

and ethereal smells that mark out a truly great wine. The 1990 is the finest Loire red I have ever drunk.

DOMAINE DU COMTE GEORGES DE VOGUE

Rue Sainte-Barbe, 21220 Chambolle-Musigny, France
Tel: (80) 62 86 25 Fax: (80) 62 62 38
Visitors: by appointment only

The main asset of this very famous *domaine* is its 16.25 acre holding of Le Musigny, the de Vogue vines accounting for three-quarters of this fabled *grand cru*. The estate also owns a sizable 6.25 acres of Bonnes Mares, 1.25 acres of the Chambolle *premier cru* Les Amoureuses, and 5 acres of straight Villages Chambolle. Given such exceptional vineyards, the estate always had the potential to produce very great red Burgundy; but for a good 20 years until the mid-1980s, the wines did not always live up to their grand reputation, sometimes lacking depth and complexity.

FACT BOX

OWNER: Baronne Elizabeth de Ladoucette

WINEMAKER: François Millet

SIZE OF VINEYARD: 30 acres

TOTAL ANNUAL PRODUCTION: 6,000 cases

GRAPE VARIETY: Pinot Noir

AVERAGE AGE OF VINES: 40 years

PERCENTAGE OF NEW WOOD: 40–70 percent depending on vintage

BEST RECENT VINTAGES: 1995, 1993, 1991

BEST DISHES TO MATCH WINES: grilled meat, venison

LOCAL RESTAURANT: Les Millesimes, Gevrey Chambertin

The nettle was grasped in 1985 when Elizabeth de Ladoucette, the present owner, appointed François Millet as the new winemaker. Radical reforms were introduced, and by the early 1990s the estate was once again among the finest on the Côte d'Or.

François likes to macerate the grapes for a long time at the end of the fermentation in order to add structure to his essentially feminine Chambolles. New wood is used sparingly. The Musigny *Vieilles Vignes* is the greatest wine in the cellar, reflecting its fabulous *terroir*. The 1991 is a magnificent example made under adverse conditions, for the estate suffered extensive hail damage that summer, resulting in a taste of dry rot in the affected grapes. So at vintage time, the story goes,

> ## TASTING NOTES
>
> ## LE MUSIGNY VIEILLES VIGNES 1992
>
> Deep extracted color for a 1992; dumb, unforthcoming nose, becoming vegetal with aeration; tannic and ungenerous both on entry and on middle palate, the fruit battling to survive. Disappointing. Last tasted September 1997. Retaste 1999.
> Rating ★

François sent 60 *vendangeurs* into the vineyard equipped with eye tweezers to pick off the split grapes. The finished wine is one of the most concentrated Musignys made at the *domaine*, quite different in style from the aromatic and relatively forward 1989. The 1992 is more problematic (see tasting note), as though the fragile fruit, typical of this high-volume vintage, was not robust enough to survive long vatting times without losing charm and aroma. Or was it in a dumb stage through which Pinot Noirs pass before revealing the gamey secondary flavors of mature Burgundy? The estate also produces a rare Musigny *blanc* in very limited quantities.

CHATEAU DUCRU BEAUCAILLOU

33250 St. Julien-Beychevelle, France
Tel: (33-5) 56 59 05 20 Fax: (33-5) 56 59 27 37
Visitors: by appointment only

*T*his property derives its name from the beautiful pebbles in the vineyard (*beaux cailloux*) and the Ducru family who owned it during the early nineteenth century. The impressive château, with its square Victorian towers joined by an elegant classical façade, is splendidly situated with commanding views over the Gironde. The 122.5-acre vineyard, bordering Beychevelle, covers the finest slopes close to the estuary. Jean-Eugène Borie, whose father bought the estate in 1941, is one of

FACT BOX

OWNER: Jean-Eugène Borie
WINEMAKER: The Borie Family
SIZE OF VINEYARD: 122.5 acres
TOTAL ANNUAL PRODUCTION:
20,000 cases
GRAPE VARIETIES: Cabernet Sauvignon
65 percent; Merlot 25 percent;
Cabernet Franc 5 percent; Petit Verdot
5 percent
AVERAGE AGE OF VINES: 30 years
PERCENTAGE OF NEW WOOD:
averaging 50 percent
BEST RECENT VINTAGES: 1996, 1990,
1986, 1982
BEST DISHES TO MATCH WINES:
roast beef and lamb, grouse
LOCAL RESTAURANTS: Le St. Julien,
St. Julien

the great gentlemen of the Medoc: modest, informative, and always in residence.

Ducru has long been famous for the elegance and breed of its wine. In a real sense it is the most classic of Medoc classed growths –fragrant, supple, but with a hidden firmness and ability to age that come from the high percentage of Cabernet Sauvignon in the *assemblage*. Ducru has a special grace and beauty of flavor in great vintages, of which there have been many. Magnificent wines were made in 1961 (now at its apogee), 1970, 1978, 1982, and 1986. The 1990 is the best Ducru, in my opinion, since the 1961 and is likely to provide perfect balanced drinking in 2005–2010. The 1994 was a great success in a respectable year, and the 1996, suffused with the flavors of very ripe Cabernet, is likely to be a very great wine for those patient, young, and healthy enough to enjoy it in 2016.

> ## TASTING NOTES
> ### CHATEAU DUCRU BEAUCAILLOU
> Beautiful, deep ruby/purple color; still tight aromas but with the promise of fragrant red fruits: very elegant, very Ducru; firm but already expressive Cabernet-dominant fruit, lovely harmony of flavors, long and fine. One of the best 1994s.
>
> Rating ★★★

In 1978, Jean-Eugène Borie purchased Château Grand Puy Lacoste in Pauillac (qv). During the last 20 years, Xavier Borie, Jean-Eugène's son, has brought this fifth growth to the front rank of classified Medoc growths. Following his father's example, he is very much a resident owner, living with his family on the property. Like the greatest chefs, the Bories do not stray far from the stove.

DOMAINE DUJAC

7 rue de la Bussière,
21220 Morey St. Denis, France
Tel: (33-3) 80 34 32 58 Fax: (33-3) 80 51 89 76
Visitors: by appointment only

As the only child of one of France's best-known gastronomes, Jacques Seysses started tasting wine at a very early age. And soon after his father had bought a share in a Volnay vineyard called La Pousse d'Or, Jacques took a month off from his Paris job to help with the harvesting and vinification of the 1966 vintage. He did the same thing the following year and his mind was made up–he wanted to buy a vineyard in Burgundy where the owner generally is his own winemaker.

In the late 1960s, Jacques finally found what he wanted, a small *domaine* in

FACT BOX

OWNER: Jacques Seysses

WINEMAKER: Jacques Seysses

SIZE OF VINEYARD: 27.5 acres

TOTAL ANNUAL PRODUCTION: 5,000 cases

GRAPE VARIETIES: Pinot Noir 95 percent; Chardonnay 5 percent

AVERAGE AGE OF VINES: 25 years

PERCENTAGE OF NEW WOOD: 80–100 percent

BEST RECENT VINTAGES: 1995, 1993, 1991, 1990, 1989

BEST DISHES TO MATCH WINES: Bresse pigeon and game birds

LOCAL RESTAURANT: Chez Greuse, Tournus

CLOS SAINT-DENIS
GRAND CRU · APPELLATION CONTRÔLÉE
1991
DOMAINE DUJAC
PROPRIÉTAIRE A MOREY-SAINT-DENIS - FRANCE
PRODUCE OF FRANCE

Domaine Dujac and its surrounding vineyards in
Morey-St. Denis.

Morey St. Denis—an old house, cellars, and 10 acres of vines. He
didn't call it Domaine Seysses, fearing that no one would be able to
pronounce, spell, or remember it. So he decided on something short
and simple, Domaine Dujac, a small play on words on his own first
name. After the *domaine* became self-supporting, in 1973 he
abandoned his job as a banker in Paris and became a full-time
vigneron with the support of his American wife, Rosalind.

The *domaine*, now considered one of the classics of the Côte de
Nuits, is currently some 27.5 acres, with sizable plots in the *grands
crus* of Clos de la Roche (4.5 acres) and Clos St. Denis (4 acres) and
smaller holdings in Bonnes Mares, Echezeaux, and some very old
vines in Gevrey Chambertin aux Combottes.

Jacques Seysses believes in very classic treatments of both the
grapes and the wine—that is, doing as little to them as possible. He
avoids pesticides and herbicides, preferring to dress his vines with
organic manure. Lasting for 10–14 days, the fermentation (and

maceration) is conducted in enameled steel vats of a size appropriate for each plot to be vinified separately. The wines are fermented

MISE AU DOMAINE

MOREY SAINT-DENIS
APPELLATION MOREY SAINT-DENIS CONTROLEE

1969

DOMAINE DUJAC
S.C.E. SEYSSES PÈRE & FILS   PROPRIÉTAIRE A MOREY - ST. DENIS (COTE D'OR)

in 100 percent new wood barrels for 16 months, yet the wines rarely taste over-oaked as the barrel staves are air-dried for three years before assembly and a light toasting.

One of the main attractions of great red Burgundy is its smell, and Dujac wines are especially aromatic. His Clos St. Denis 1972 (a vastly underrated vintage), drunk in 1988, was a superbly spicy and sensual wine, a real little "Jesus in velvet pants," as they say in Beaune. The Clos de la Roche is more substantial, a sleeper for the long march and particularly so in the small-crop 1991 vintage, one of the best-kept Burgundy secrets of recent years.

TASTING NOTES

CLOS DE LA ROCHE, DOMAINE DUJAC, 1991

A deeper than usual color for a Dujac wine, a true "robe"; intense, concentrated Pinot Noir fruit with secondary aromas of minerals, spice, and leather; superb texture coats the mouth, powerful yet ripe tannins and a complex interplay of flavors, animal, vegetable, and mineral. The end flavor lasts a good two minutes. *Grand vin.* Drink from 2000. Rating ★★★★★

ANGELO GAJA

Via Torino 36, 12050 Barbaresco (CN), Italy
Tel: (0039) 173 63 51 58 Fax: (0039) 173 63 52 56
Visitors: strictly by appointment

*T*he Gaja family came from Spain and settled in Piedmont in the mid-seventeenth century. In 1859, Giovanni Gaja established the winery, and it is his great-grandson Angelo who, since 1961, has transformed a traditional Barbaresco wine business into one of Italy's most prestigious estates. A single-vineyard Barbaresco from Gaja now costs as much as a super-second-growth claret or a *grand cru* Burgundy, which is a tribute to this extraordinary man's promotional flair.

Gaja's commitment to the highest standards of winemaking is total, but he has

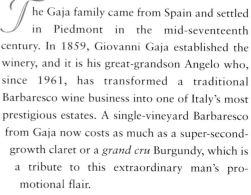

FACT BOX

OWNER: Gaja Societa Semplice

WINEMAKER: Angelo Gaja

SIZE OF VINEYARD: 225 acres

TOTAL ANNUAL PRODUCTION: 32,000 cases

GRAPE VARIETIES: Nebbiolo 48 percent; Barbera, Dolcetto, and Freisa 32 percent; non-indigenous varieties 20 percent

AVERAGE AGE OF VINES: 30 years (Barbaresco vineyards)

PERCENTAGE OF NEW WOOD: 33–50 percent

BEST RECENT VINTAGES: 1990, 1989, 1988

BEST DISHES TO MATCH WINES: game and porcini mushrooms

TASTING NOTES

GAJA
BARBARESCO 1990

Elegant, deep-ruby color, lovely Barbaresco nose of tar and roses; beautifully defined Nebbiolo fruit, rich and full, no hint of oxidized flavors. Very long finish. Exemplary.

Rating ★★★

always realized that a wine is only as good as the grapes from which it is made. In the mid-1960s, he pioneered a pruning system that radically reduced the yields of the Nebbiolo grape by restricting growth to 10 buds per vine. With the arrival of Guido Rivella, Gaja's oenologist, in the 1970s, a greater purity of fruit and softer tannins were apparent in the wine. This considerable advance was achieved by the use of nitrogen during vinification, which protected the wine from oxidation and volatile acidity, the two main faults of old-style Barbaresco.

Gaja's three single-vineyard Barbarescos are world-class wines. The Sori San Lorenzo (9.75 acres) is well-balanced yet deeply flavored; the Sori Russi (11 acres) is splendidly aromatic with a velvet-like texture that recalls a great burgundy; the Sori Tilden (8.5 acres) has the deepest color, the most durable structure, and the greatest capacity to age. For a more reasonably priced wine, the straight Barbaresco 1990 is a fine example from a great year.

Gaja additionally makes impressive Barolo from his 70-acre Marenca-Rivette vineyard at Serralunga. He was also the first grower to plant Cabernet Sauvignon (and Chardonnay) in Piedmont. The wines are undeniably excellent, especially the 1991 Darmagi Cabernet Sauvignon, though prices are stiff.

Angelo Gaja, winemaker extraordinaire.

ETABLISSEMENTS GUIGAL

Château d'Ampuis, 69420 Ampuis, France
Tel: (33-4) 74 56 10 22 Fax: (33-4) 74 56 28 76
Visitors: by appointment only

*M*arcel Guigal is the pivotal figure of the northern Rhône, a man who through a combination of brilliant winemaking and an astute sense of the market has taught the outside world that Côte Rôtie is as fine a wine as any red Bordeaux or Burgundy. The firm was founded in

FACT BOX

OWNERS: Guigal family

WINEMAKER: Marcel Guigal

SIZE OF VINEYARD: Château d'Ampuis (20.25 acres); Brune et Blonde (20.25 acres); La Mouline (3.55 acres); La Landonne (4.27 acres); La Turque (2.5 acres)

TOTAL ANNUAL PRODUCTION: Château d'Ampuis (2,300 cases); Brune et Blonde (1,650 cases); La Mouline (400 cases); La Landonne (800 cases); La Turque (400 cases)

GRAPE VARIETIES: Syrah 89–100 percent; Viognier 0–11 percent (depending on wine)

AVERAGE AGE OF VINES: from 15 years (La Turque) to 70 years (La Mouline)

PERCENTAGE OF NEW WOOD: up to 100 percent

BEST RECENT VINTAGES: 1995, 1991, 1990, 1988

BEST DISHES TO MATCH WINES: venison, daube of beef, roasted game birds

LOCAL RESTAURANTS: Beau Rivage, Condrieu; Pyramide, Vienne

1946 by his father, Etienne
Guigal, the former cellar master
and vineyard manager of the old
house of Vidal Fleury in Ampuis.
Marcel became manager of the
company in 1971; 26 years later
it remains a tight-knit family
business. The administration is
ably run by Marcel's wife
Bernadette, and his son, another
Etienne, will be the winemaker
for the future.

Guigal's three top single-vineyard Côte Rôties (La Mouline, La
Landonne, and La Turque) are magnificently rich and sensuous
expressions of mature Syrah, harvested late, long vatted, and aged
for 42 months in 100 percent new oak. The downside is that owing
to their scarcity (just 1,600 cases in total of the three *crus* for all
world markets) and the lavish praise heaped on them by American

Guigal's vineyards, typically crisscrossed with
terraces to keep the vines and soil in place.

Château Guigal situated on the narrow
Rhône Valley corridor.

critics, they cost the earth and are virtually unobtainable. Côte
Rôtie lovers on a budget should look to Guigal's splendid "Brune
et Blonde" bottling, a surefire success, especially in the 1988 and
1991 vintages. For future drinking, the new Château d'Ampuis,
first released in 1995, gives you a taste of the Guigal magic at a
relatively affordable price. And his exemplary Côtes du Rhône is
one of the finest values of classic French wines.

CHATEAU HAUT-BRION

B.P. 24 33602 Pessac, Bordeaux, France
Tel: (33-5) 56 00 29 30 Fax: (33-5) 56 98 75 14
Visitors: by appointment

*O*f all the first growths of Bordeaux, Haut-Brion is the real charmer, always elegant and refined, never out of sorts, showing well young or old. It is also the senior and historically most colorful wine estate of the Gironde, the first single-vineyard claret to be sold outside France in the coffeehouses of seventeenth-century London and drunk to rave notices by such Restoration diarists as Samuel Pepys and John Evelyn. Daniel Defoe, John Locke, and Jonathan Swift all admired the wine. And that arch-trimmer Talleyrand owned the property briefly,

FACT BOX

OWNER: SA Domaine Clarence Dillon
WINEMAKER: Jean-Bernard Delmas
SIZE OF VINEYARD: 107.5 acres
SECOND WINE: Château Bahans
TOTAL ANNUAL PRODUCTION:
16,000 cases
GRAPE VARIETIES: Cabernet Sauvignon
45 percent; Cabernet Franc 18 percent;
Merlot 37 percent
AVERAGE AGE OF VINES: 35 years
PERCENTAGE OF NEW WOOD:
100 percent
BEST RECENT VINTAGES: 1995, 1990,
1989, 1986, 1982
BEST DISHES TO MATCH WINES:
red meats and game
LOCAL RESTAURANTS: Le Chapon Fin,
Jean Ramet; both in Bordeaux

though he seemed never to have visited the charming turreted manor house on the outskirts of Bordeaux.

In 1935, the property was bought by Clarence Dillon, the American banker, who invested large sums in the renovation of the *chai* and vineyard. His granddaughter Joan, the Duchesse de Mouchy, is now president of the enterprise, her long-serving general manager, Jean-Bernard Delmas, one of the ablest winemakers in Bordeaux. In 1960, on his initiative, Haut-Brion was the first *premier cru* to replace the old wood fermenting tuns with stainless-steel tanks. Delmas has also been a leader of research in Bordeaux grape varieties and clones, having established an important vine nursery on the estate. The Dillon family acquired next-door Château la Mission Haut Brion (qv) in 1983.

> ## TASTING NOTES
> ### CHATEAU HAUT-BRION 1989
>
> Atypically a huge wine of immense concentration. Very deep purple; multitoned bouquet of blackcurrant, "cigar-box" and tobacco leaf; lanolin texture, great wells of fruit in perfect balance with ripe tannins. A very great wine. Good until 2020 at least. Rating ★★★★★

Haut-Brion is almost invariably the most forward and approachable of the first growths, but this easy, early charm is deceptive, for the wine ages beautifully. The 1975 and 1979 are only now approaching their apogee, and that remarkable clutch of vintages–1982, 1983, 1985, and 1986–is still well short of full maturity. The 1989 Haut-Brion is the red wine of the vintage, eclipsing Lafite, Latour, and Margaux by any measure of wine excellence, and a worthy successor to the magnificent 1959.

C. A. HENSCHKE

P.O. Box 100, Keyneton, 5353 Australia
Tel: (08) 8564 8223 Fax: (08) 8294
Visitors: Monday–Friday 9AM–4PM; Saturday 9AM–NOON

The village of Keyneton, located high in the Barossa Ranges, was named after Joseph Keynes, the first settler in the district. Keyneton played a major role in the early pioneering days of the Australian wine industry. Seven wineries were already established there before 1900; almost 100 years later, Henschke is the greatest estate in the district and, most would say, in all Australia.

The Henschke family, which is of German and Polish origin, produce a superb range of both white and red wines. Their main Eden Valley vineyards are located in cooler and

FACT BOX

OWNERS: Stephen and Prue Henschke
WINEMAKER: Stephen Henschke
SIZE OF VINEYARD: 250 acres in Eden Valley, Barossa Valley, and Adelaide Hills
TOTAL ANNUAL PRODUCTION: 600 tons
GRAPE VARIETIES: Shiraz 30 percent; Cabernet Sauvignon 10 percent; Merlot 3 percent; Malbec 2 percent; remaining 55 percent Riesling, Chardonnay, Semillon, Sauvignon Blanc, and Gewürztraminer
AVERAGE AGE OF VINES: 50 years
PERCENTAGE OF NEW WOOD: 70 percent French, 30 percent American
BEST RECENT VINTAGE: 1990
BEST DISHES TO MATCH WINES: beef, veal, pork, game, lamb

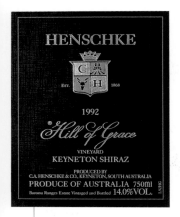

higher sites than those of the hot Barossa Valley floor. This climatic advantage allows the Henschkes to make aromatic Sauvignon/Semillon, luscious Rhine Riesling, and subtle Cabernet Sauvignon. But their greatest wine is undoubtedly the sonorously named Hill of Grace, made from Shiraz vines brought from Europe by the early German settlers in the 1840s. A Polish forbear of the family, Nicolaus Stanitski later planted the vines near the winery,

opposite a beautiful old Lutheran church. The vines, which are now up to 130 years old, yield very small crops of grapes with an extraordinary intensity of flavor.

You might think that the wine-making would be highly traditional and based on long vatting times. This is not the case, for Stephen Henschke is an innovative maker of Shiraz who wants to wring something special from his remarkable fruit and vineyard. The "cap" is submerged for just seven days, and the wine is drawn off while the skins are still fermenting. In this way, the

TASTING NOTES

HENSCHKE HILL OF GRACE, KEYNETON SHIRAZ 1992

Lovely seamless appearance, a deep, dark ruby, no hint of age at rim; ripe mulberry fruit of the highest class on nose and palate melds with mineral flavors of great complexity. Silky texture, yet very persistent in the mouth. A near-faultless wine. Rating ★★★★

lovely, soft Shiraz tannins are preserved and the wine derives its complexity, concentration, and longevity from the age of the vines. This is one of the great red wines of the world, but with a softness and charm that is inimitably Australian and a tribute to the lightness of touch of its maker.

"Hill of Grace" vineyard at Henschke where the Shiraz vines are over 100 years old.

MAISON LOUIS JADOT

21 rue Spullier, 21200 Beaune, France
Tel: (33-3) 80 20 10 57 Fax: (33-3) 80 22 56 03
Visitors: by appointment only

*M*aison Louis Jadot is the bluest of blue-chip Beaune firms and also the most profitable. The purchase of the company in the mid-1980s by the Koch sisters, owners of its American distributor, Kobrand, was a takeover with a difference, for it has turned out to be wholly beneficial to Burgundy. The Gagey family (André and now his son Pierre Henri), who have run the firm for 30 years, crucially sold from a position of strength because Kobrand wanted to protect the plum Jadot agency from rival U.S. bidders. As a result, the Gageys, supported by the new American finance, were given–and

FACT BOX

OWNERS: Koch family (Kobrand)
WINEMAKER: Jacques Lardiere
SIZE OF VINEYARD: 6.25 acres
TOTAL ANNUAL PRODUCTION: 800 to 1,100 cases
GRAPE VARIETY: Pinot Noir
AVERAGE AGE OF VINES: 35–40 years
PERCENTAGE OF NEW WOOD: 25 percent
BEST RECENT VINTAGES: 1996, 1995, 1993, 1990
BEST DISHES TO MATCH WINES: Bresse hen with morel mushrooms; jugged hare
LOCAL RESTAURANTS: Le Jardin des Remparts, Beaune; Lameloise, Chagny

retain—a free hand in managing the company; they have since significantly extended its vineyards in the finest sites, especially in the top red *crus* of the Côte de Nuits.

The estate is now some 105 acres and includes some outstanding plots in Clos de Vougeot (8 acres) and Corton-Pougets (3.85 acres). There is a beautiful new winery in Beaune, first used for the 1997 vintage, where Jacques Lardiere, a winemaker of genius, works his magic. A total of 130 top-flight, richly flavored reds and magnificent long-lived whites are produced, all from Burgundy without exception. A Corton (Dr. Peste) 1990 bottled by Jadot is the best wine from the great hill I have ever tasted.

With such an embarrassment of riches, this profile focuses on one of the firm's most reliable and reasonably priced wines, the monopole Beaune Clos des Ursules. As its name implies, this is an enclosed 6.25 acre vineyard of excellent east-facing aspect, 891 feet high, within the *appellation* of Beaune Premier Cru Vignes Franches. The Pinot Noir vines are of good age (35 to 40 years). Fermentation and maceration lasts for four weeks in open wooden vats, after which the wine matures for 20 months in oak barrels (25 percent new wood) before bottling. All these factors contribute to a sturdy classic Beaune of deep rich color, frank aromas, and well-defined flavors faithful to its origins. If I had to choose a fine red Burgundy I could absolutely rely on to deliver body, balance, quality, and value on the proverbial desert island, this would be it. Of four cracking vintages in the nineties (1990, 1993, 1995, and 1996), the 1993 is the most classic, destined for a long, distinguished life.

> ## TASTING NOTES
> ### BEAUNE CLOS DES URSULES 1993
>
> Rich, bright, elegant ruby; firm, tight nose; the aromas of top-flight Pinot are potentially all there, but this is a wine holding a lot in reserve; firm and sturdy on the palate but with a beautiful flavor definition of fruit, discreet oak, and a long, vinous finish. Drink from 1999.
> Rating ★★★★

DOMAINE ROBERT JASMIN

Côte Rôtie, 69420 Ampuis, France
Tel: (33-4) 74 56 11 44 Fax: (33-4) 74 56 01 78
Visitors: by appointment

*R*obert Jasmin is everyone's idea of a French winegrower: large, jovial, and full of *joie de vivre*. His relaxed approach to life is mirrored in his Côte Rôtie, which is made with a light touch and is among the most perfumed and subtle of the *appellation*. Robert's wife Josette is a model of common sense who has worked in a local factory for many years to keep the family finances on an even keel.

The *domaine* was founded by Robert's grandfather, who came from Champagne in the 1930s to cook at the Château d'Ampuis. Today there are 9.75 acres of

FACT BOX

OWNER: Robert Jasmin
WINEMAKER: Robert Jasmin
SIZE OF VINEYARD: 9.75 acres
TOTAL ANNUAL PRODUCTION:
1,500 cases
GRAPE VARIETIES: Syrah 95 percent;
Viognier 5 percent
AVERAGE AGE OF VINES: 35 years
PERCENTAGE OF NEW WOOD:
10 percent
BEST RECENT VINTAGES: 1995, 1991,
1990, 1988, 1983, 1978
BEST DISHES TO MATCH WINES:
Jugged hare, daube of wild boar
LOCAL HOTEL/RESTAURANT: Beau
Rivage, Condrieu; La Pyramide, Vienne

mature vines situated mainly on the feruginous mica-schist soils of the best Côte Brune hillsides, so ideal for growing great Syrah. There is nothing high-tech about this cellar. The wines are made in the old way, *à la facon de grandpère.* Grapes are not destemmed and fermentations in cement vats last for 15–20 days. The wines are then matured in a mixture of 156-gallon *demi-muids* casks and 58.5-gallon *pièces* for up to two years. Robert believes that the unbridled use of new oak is standardizing French wines, so brand new barrels only account for 10 percent of the total in his cellar.

> ## TASTING NOTES
> ## CÔTE ROTIE 1995
> Lovely, deep, clear and elegant ruby; fragrant scent of raspberry and earthier smell of truffles, classic Côte Rôtie; tender, pure Syrah fruit, exquisite balance and length. *Grand vin.* Drink from 2003.
> Rating ★★★★

The results are sensuous, finely wrought wines, not heavy or overextracted, and are in a real sense the Chambolle Musignys of Côte Rôtie. The 1995 is an exceptional wine (*see* Tasting Notes), as was the 1991. The legendary 1978, a collector's item, is magnificent, a wine of poised balance and concentration, the surging Syrah fruit still vitally fresh at 20 years of age.

Robert Jasmin, maker of the exceptional
Côte Rôtie.

DOMAINE MICHEL LAFARGE

Rue de la Combe, 21190 Volnay, France
Tel: (33-3) 80 21 61 61 Fax: (33-3) 80 21 67 83
Visitors: by appointment only

Despite the big advances in winemaking that occurred on the Côte d'Or during the late 1980s and early 1990s, buying classic red Burgundy is still a chancy exercise. Yet if one had to name a grower whose every wine is consistently excellent, it would have to be Michel Lafarge, the former mayor of Volnay.

A tall, distinguished, and contemplative man in his early seventies, Lafarge started life with distinct advantages. The family

FACT BOX

OWNER: Michel Lafarge

WINEMAKER: Michel and Frederic Lafarge

SIZE OF VINEYARD: 26.62 acres

TOTAL ANNUAL PRODUCTION: 6,000 cases

GRAPE VARIETIES: Pinor Noir 95 percent; Chardonnay 5 percent

AVERAGE AGE OF VINES: 30 years

PERCENTAGE OF NEW WOOD: information not available

BEST RECENT VINTAGES: 1996, 1995, 1993, 1990

BEST BUY: 1992

BEST DISHES TO MATCH WINES: roasted, lightly hung game birds such as partridge; also Bresse pigeon

domaine, founded in the nineteenth century, was one of the first estates to bottle its wines in the 1930s. The Lafarges' prize possession is their 2¼-acre parcel of Clos des Chenes, which consistently produces their finest, most ageworthy wine; the perfume and bouquet of great Volnay is allied to a magical mix of supreme refinement and a substantial tannic structure to ensure a very long life. The 1983, drunk in 1994, is one of the best four or five wines I have ever encountered in 30 years of enthusiastic tasting. Other gems in this cellar are the frankly expressive and beautifully balanced Beaune Grèves, the upright and elegant Pommard Pezerolles, and the majestically fruity Volnay Clos du Château des Ducs, a monopole that had been leased out for many years but returned to the family in the late 1980s. All these are fabulous wines, on strict allocation, and very expensive.

Yet the masterly winemaking of Michel and his son Frederic is as exhilerating in their less famous wines. The modestly labeled Bourgogne rouge is in all but official status a delicious mini-Volnay, and the Volnay Vendanges Selectionnes is a star buy, better than other growers' *premiers crus* in the generally average vintages of 1992 and 1994. The Lafarges also make a little white Meursault, all the more charming for not being over-oaked.

Michel Lafarge is one of the most open-minded winemakers on the Côte, always ready to discuss a fine Pinot Noir or Chardonnay from California on its own merits. For him, vinification is observation, requiring a flexible approach based on his very long experience of the climatic twists and turns of Volnay at harvest time. Every year is different, every year he delivers the goods.

TASTING NOTES

VOLNAY DOMAINE MICHEL LAFARGE 1992

Fine example of the master's touch in a light, often dilute year for red Burgundy. Good sustained but elegant red color, pure full Volnay fruit with touches of spice and game; acidity and moderate tannins make it ideal to drink now or keep a little (1999–2001).

Rating ★★★

CHATEAU LAFITE-ROTHSCHILD

33250 Pauillac, France
Tel: (33-5) 56 73 18 18 Fax: (33-5) 56 59 26 83
Visitors: strictly by appointment

*T*he *ne plus ultra* of Bordeaux châteaux and the most prestigious wine estate in the world, Lafite at first sight appears to be the most serene and discreet of the First Growths. The château itself is a delightful seventeenth-century manor house, the intimate scale of the public rooms and bedrooms creating the atmosphere of a lived-in

FACT BOX

OWNERS: Domaines des Barons Rothschild

WINEMAKER: Gilbert Rokvam

SIZE OF VINEYARD: 235 acres

SECOND WINE: Carruades de Lafite

TOTAL ANNUAL PRODUCTION: 20,000 cases (*grand vin*)

GRAPE VARIETIES: Cabernet Sauvignon 70 percent; Merlot 20 percent; Cabernet Franc 10 percent

AVERAGE AGE OF VINES: 40 years

PERCENTAGE OF NEW WOOD: 100 percent

BEST RECENT VINTAGES: 1996, 1995, 1990, 1988, 1983, 1982

BEST DISHES TO MATCH WINES: simple roasts of the finest beef and lamb

LOCAL HOTEL/RESTAURANT: Château Cordeillan Bages, Pauillac

country house. Yet behind its timeless façade, a quiet revolution has been taking place at Lafite during the last 25 years.

When Baron Eric de Rothschild took over responsibility for the château in 1974, the reputation of the wines was at a low ebb after a succession of indifferent vintages in the 1960s and early 1970s. Baron Eric lost no time in calling in Professor Emile Peynaud, the dean of Bordeaux oenologists, to advise. A new winemaking team under Jean Crete (ex Leoville-Las-Cases) was appointed in 1975. In 1983, Gilbert Rokvam succeeded Crete and introduced further improvements, such as reducing the time the wines spend in cask in frailer vintages, a crucial decision that succeeded in restoring the vividness of fruit that Lafite had lacked for far too long. A new second-year *chai* of striking circular design was completed in 1987, followed 12 months later by a new winery equipped with temperature-controlled stainless-steel vats.

> ### TASTING NOTES
> #### CHATEAU LAFITE-ROTHSCHILD 1990
> A complete wine that has everything: superb, shimmering ruby color; complex, classic nose of blackcurrant, cedar, and a judicious touch of vanilla, flavors at once powerful and refined; destined for a long life. Drink from 2010. Rating ★★★★★

Since the coming of Eric de Rothschild, vintages at Lafite have refound their verve and elegance, allied to an increasing depth of color, opulence, and intensity of flavor. The 1975 was the first great Lafite since 1959. The 1982 and 1983 are durably structured, superb wines, some years away from maturity, which are an interesting corrective to the old wisdom that Lafite is always delicate. The 1990 is a personal favorite, charm and power in perfect balance, while the fragrant 1995 and muscular 1996 bode well for the future. Since 1985, a much more rigorous selection of the wines for the *grand vin* has been applied, a larger proportion of the crop going into the second wine, Carruades de Lafite, which is correspondingly very much improved.

LAKE'S FOLLY VINEYARDS

Broke Road, Pokolbin 2320, NSW, Australia
Tel: (02) 4998 7307 Fax: (02) 4998 7322
Visitors: Monday–Saturday 10:00AM–4:00PM

When Max Lake, a Sydney hand surgeon, decided in 1963 to plant Cabernet vines in the steamy Hunter Valley, everyone told him he was mad. Being a tough-minded, unsquashable fellow, Max took no notice, as he was convinced he had found the perfect spot at Pokolbin. The *terroir* (total natural environment) of the vineyard that he wryly christened "Lake's Folly" offered a rare combination of volcanic hill, alluvial creek flat, and southeasterly aspect. The Cabernet vines are now over 30 years old, giving greater depth of flavor to the wines of a classic estate long known fondly as Australia's first "boutique winery," and one whose influence has been out of all

FACT BOX

OWNER: Dr. Max Lake

WINEMAKER: Stephen Lake

SIZE OF VINEYARD: 30 acres

TOTAL ANNUAL PRODUCTION:
3,000 cases

GRAPE VARIETY: Cabernet Sauvignon
(for red wines)

AVERAGE AGE OF VINES: 30 years+

PERCENTAGE OF NEW WOOD:
33 percent

BEST RECENT VINTAGES: 1996, 1994,
1993, 1987

BEST DISHES TO MATCH WINES:
red meats and game

proportion to its size. The advantage of being small allows the Lakes to select each block of grapes at their peak and pick them when they are cool, early in the day.

Given excellent fruit, the wine-making is classical. The reds are open fermented, with gentle treatment of the cap in the most traditional manner. This gives softer tannins and makes the finished wines more approachable. Efficient cooling is the main concession to technology. After fermentation – the

time on the skins varies from seven to 20 days depending on the character of the vintage–the wine goes directly into old casks for natural settling. The following spring it is transferred into smaller new French oak *barriques* for 18 months before bottling. Soft and naturally elegant, Lake's Folly Cabernet Sauvignon can be drunk young but also ages significantly better than most Australian wines of its type. The list of excellent years is long, 1987, 1981, and 1978 being outstanding; the latter was cellared by

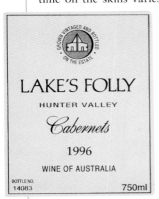

the Michelin three-star restaurant Les Trois Gros in 1990. More recently, the 1996 made by Stephen Lake, Max's son, is also exceptional. The estate also makes an excellent Chardonnay in a firm, well-structured style.

Max Lake (right) and his son Stephen.

CHATEAU LA MISSION-HAUT-BRION

33400 Talence Bordeaux, France
Tel: (33-5) 56 00 29 30 Fax: (33-5) 56 98 75 14
Visitors: by appointment

*I*n the seventeenth century, the *domaine* of la Mission-Haut-Brion was bequeathed to the Pères Lazaristes, a religious order founded by St. Vincent de Paul. For the next hundred years until the French Revolution of 1789, the fathers strove to make this good red wine of the Graves into something remarkable; the story goes that they preached *sotto voce* sermons to the soil to encourage the birth of even riper grapes. A little "mission" chapel still stands on the site. For much of the twentieth century, the estate was owned and managed in

FACT BOX

OWNER: Domaine Clarence Dillon
WINEMAKER: Jean-Bernard Delmas
SIZE OF VINEYARD: 42.5 acres
TOTAL ANNUAL PRODUCTION: 7,000 cases
GRAPE VARIETIES: Cabernet Sauvignon 48 percent; Merlot 45 percent; Cabernet Franc 7 percent
AVERAGE AGE OF VINES: 19 years
PERCENTAGE OF NEW WOOD: 100 percent
BEST RECENT VINTAGES: 1995, 1990, 1989, 1988, 1986, 1985
BEST DISHES TO MATCH WINES: roast grouse and venison
LOCAL RESTAURANTS: Le Chapon Fin, Jean Ramet; both in Bordeaux

exemplary fashion by the Woltner family, passionate vintners, who established the international reputation of the wine. Since 1983, the estate has belonged to the Dillon family of Haut-Brion. Under Jean-Bernard Delmas' enlightened management, the old *chai* has been modernized and a significant part of the vineyard replanted with Merlot from the healthiest rootstock.

The wine of La Mission is deeply colored and packs more of a punch than Haut-Brion; warm flavored with an ironlike strength, it is both rich and intense without being either harsh or overblown. The concentration of the wine has a lot to do with the exceptional depth of gravel in the vineyard and the low yields. A remarkable sequence of top-flight wines was made at La Mission in 1981, 1982, 1983, 1985, 1986, 1988, 1989, and 1990. The 1995 is spectacular. This is a First Growth in all but name, reflected in its high price. The white Graves of Château Laville Haut-Brion is also made here.

> ## TASTING NOTES
> ### CHATEAU LA MISSION-HAUT-BRION 1990
> Slower maturing than the 1990 Haut-Brion, a classic La Mission; still deep, dark ruby; exotic bouquet of warm earth, leather, and pepper; powerful tannic presence on the palate but in balance with superb fruit and extract. Drink from 2003.
> Rating ★★★★

CHÂTEAU LATOUR

33250 Pauillac, France
Tel: (33-5) 56 73 19 80 Fax: (33-5) 56 73 19 81
Visitors: by appointment

*C*hâteau Latour takes its name from the original square stone tower (depicted on the label) that was a defense fort against marauding pirates during the Middle Ages. The vineyard, which dates essentially from the sixteenth century, lies at the extreme southern point of the Pauillac *appellation*, on a high bank of gravel overlooking the Gironde estuary and separated from neighboring Leoville-Las-Cases by a small stream.

The de Beaumont family owned the property for 300 years until a British syndicate, headed by Lord Cowdray and

FACT BOX

OWNER: François Pinault

WINEMAKER: information not available

SIZE OF VINEYARD: 107.5 acres

SECOND WINE: Les Forts de Latour

TOTAL ANNUAL PRODUCTION: 20,000 cases (*grand vin*)

GRAPE VARIETIES: Cabernet Sauvignon 80 percent; Merlot 15 percent; Cabernet Franc 4 percent; Petit Verdot 1 percent

AVERAGE AGE OF VINES: 35 years

PERCENTAGE OF NEW WOOD: 100 percent

BEST RECENT VINTAGES: 1996, 1994, 1990

BEST DISHES TO MATCH WINES: venison, jugged hare, grouse

LOCAL HOTEL/RESTAURANT: Château Cordeillan-Bages, Pauillac

Harveys of Bristol, bought a majority share in 1963. On the advice of the great British wine authority Harry Waugh, stainless-steel fermenters were quickly introduced to replace the old wooden vats–an innovation that raised the eyebrows of the conservative Bordelais. They soon changed their tune after tasting the new 1964 Latour, which was acclaimed as the best wine of the vintage. After briefly passing through the hands of Allied Lyons, Latour returned to French ownership in 1993, when it was acquired by the industrialist, François Pinault.

The old tower at Château Latour.

Latour back on top form and typically outclassing the opposing in an average, though useful, year. Great purple-black color, gorgeous scents of little red fruits; mouthfilling and generous, swathed for the moment in the vanilla tones of new oak, but with beautifully ripe tannins and an endlessly long finish. Drink 2005–20.
Last tasted November 1997.
Rating ★★★★

For many years Latour has been rated by top critics as the greatest of all clarets. Massive, uncompromisingly tannic, intense, with a brilliant counterpoint of flavors ranging from blackcurrant and black cherry to licorice and bay leaf, it is the marathon runner of Bordeaux wines; great years like 1945 and 1947 are still athletic and full of zip at 50 years of age. Similarly superb wines were made in 1949, 1959, 1961, 1962, 1966, 1970, 1975, 1978, and 1982. However, Latour then lost its way a little, with a particularly weedy and diffuse 1983 that seemed to signal a misguided move to make the wines lighter and softer. Fortunately, Latour appears to have returned to majestic form with a brilliant 1990 and a reassuringly powerful 1994, the first vintage made entirely under the new ownership.

The first year cellar at Château Latour. Wines are aged for up to 35 years.

DOMAINE LEROY

21700, Vosne-Romanée, France
Tel: (33-3) 80 61 10 82 Fax: (33-3) 80 21 63 81
Visitors: strictly by appointment

*B*ritish and American wine critics do not always see eye to eye about Burgundy. Yet there is general agreement on both sides of the Atlantic that, of all the leading red winemakers on the Côte, Madame Lalou Bize-Leroy is the brightest star. This elfin lady's more prestigious wines sell for $500 a bottle. But sell they do, demonstrating that there is always a market for outstanding wines at high prices.

The Domaine Leroy was founded from the initial purchase of the vineyards and buildings of the moribund Domaine Charles Noellat of Vosne-Romanée in April 1988, and from those of Philippe Remy's estate in Gevrey Chambertin the

FACT BOX

OWNER: Maison Leroy
WINEMAKER: André Porcheret
SIZE OF VINEYARD: 56 acres
TOTAL ANNUAL PRODUCTION: 8,000 cases
GRAPE VARIETY: Pinot Noir
AVERAGE AGE OF VINES: 40 years
PERCENTAGE OF NEW WOOD: 100 percent
BEST RECENT VINTAGES: 1993, 1990
BEST DISHES TO MATCH WINES: grilled red and white meats, game
RESTAURANTS: L'Arpège, L'Ambroisie, Carré des Feuillants, Paris; Le Cirque, Le Montrachet, New York

following year. Lalou was particularly enthusiastic about the quality of the Noellat holdings in Romanée St. Vivant and Richebourg. But she was very slow to acknowledge that these plots conflicted directly with vineyards owned by the Domaine de la Romanée-Conti, of which she was a codirector at the time. It all ended in tears in 1991, when she was ousted from the board of the DRC.

With a new freedom to do what she pleased, Lalou quickly decided that the cultivation of the Leroy vines should go over to biodynamic methods, and she rapidly built up the *domaine* by further purchases in the finest sites, notably choice plots in Le Musigny, Clos de la Roche, Corton Renardes, and a full 3.12 acres of Pommard Les Vignots. From an initial base of 30 acres in 1988, the Domaine Leroy had nearly doubled in size to 56 acres by 1997. In the vineyards yields are kept very low, though they naturally vary from vintage

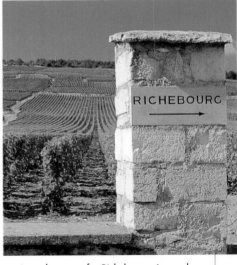

A marker stone for Richebourg vineyard at Vosne-Romanée.

to vintage. Winemaking is very classical but with ingenious modern touches. For example, the grapes are not destemmed, and though the lengthy fermentations take place *à l'ancienne* in open-topped wooden vats, these have been equipped with stainless-steel temperature controllers placed near their bases, an idea developed from the early work of the great Alsace grower-winemaker, Leonard Humbrecht. The wines then go into 100 percent new oak made from staves first weathered in the open air for three years. The results are a range of the most stunning red wines in Burgundy: deep-colored, intense, rich, but with a true variety of flavors faithful to their originating villages and vineyards. Lalou's favorite vintage to date is 1993, a problem child that has turned out to be a small but perfectly formed young adult. The Romanée St. Vivant of that year is probably her greatest wine, though the best buy is the Vosne Romanée Les Beaumonts.

TASTING NOTES

ROMANEE ST VIVANT 1993

Deep concentrated ruby, yet bright and elegant; great ethereal Vosne nose, old-vines Pinot fruit, Asian spices; magnificent silky texture, mouth-coating, very complex secondary flavors, animal, vegetable and mineral; incredibly long finish, stays with you for four or five minutes.

Rating ★★★★★

Chateau Lynch-Bages

B.P. 120, 33250 Pauillac, France
Tel: (33-5) 56 73 24 00 Fax: (33-5) 56 59 26 42
Visitors: Monday–Friday
Summer 9:30AM–12:30PM and 2:00PM–7:00PM
Winter 9:00AM–12:00 NOON and 2:00PM–6:00PM

*L*ynch-Bages, a charming but unassuming house, lies midway between Mouton and Lafite on a plateau called Bages, just southwest of the sleepy town of Pauillac on the Gironde estuary. The vineyards formed part of the lands of Lafite in the sixteenth and seventeenth centuries, but it was not until 1728 that the first archives record the purchase of the property by Pierre Drouillard,

FACT BOX

OWNER: Jean-Michel Cazes
WINEMAKER: Daniel Llose
SIZE OF VINEYARD: 225 acres
SECOND LABEL: Château Haut-Bages Averous
TOTAL ANNUAL PRODUCTION: 35,000 cases
GRAPE VARIETIES: Cabernet Sauvignon 75 percent; Merlot 25 percent; Cabernet Franc 10 percent
AVERAGE AGE OF VINES: 35 years
PERCENTAGE OF NEW WOOD: up to 75 percent (depending on vintage)
BEST RECENT VINTAGES: 1996, 1995, 1990, 1989, 1988
BEST BUY: 1994
BEST DISHES TO MATCH WINES: red meats (especially Pauillac lamb), and game
LOCAL HOTEL/RESTAURANT: Château Cordeillan-Bages (Relais et Châteaux), Pauillac

The house is situated just southwest of the town of
Pauillac on the Gironde estuary.

a Bordeaux dignitary. His daughter and heir, Elizabeth, married
into the Lynch family, who had come to Bordeaux from Ireland.
The property was bought in 1937 by Jean-Charles Cazes, the
grandfather of the current owner, Jean-Michel Cazes. Before
acquiring Lynch-Bages, Jean-Charles Cazes had already learned his
craft as the highly respect winemaker and proprietor of the St.
Estèphe *cru bourgeois* Château Les Ormes de Pez (still owned by
the Cazes family).

Lynch-Bages in the 1940s and 1950s is a story of perfectionism.
Jean-Charles made some magnificent vintages that, if they have
been well cellared, are still drinking well today. The classic, beautifully balanced 1955 and the powerful and intense 1947 are outstanding examples cited by Clive Coates in his authoritative *Grands
Vins* (Weidenfeld and Nicolson). My first experience of very great
claret was the powerful and cedary 1961, drunk in 1976. The 1962
is another great wine.

During the 1970s, the quality of Lynch-Bages declined, and the
wines became lighter and less complex. The reasons were the usual
ones afflicting many estates in France. Jean-Charles died in 1972 at
the age of 95 and his son André was faced with a huge inheritance
tax bill; there was little spare cash to modernize winemaking equip-

ment, the cellar staff were aging and set in their ways. But André Cazes, a local politician of agile mind and quick wit, shrewdly appointed a brilliant young winemaker, Daniel Llose, in 1976. Llose's talent was given full rein in the early 1980s with the completion of a redesigned cellar-house that included stainless-steel, temperature controlled fermenters and, crucially, more space to separately vinify the grapes from different parcels of the vineyard. The full concentrated 1981 was the first tangible evidence of the reborn Lynch-Bages, followed by the magnificent 1982. The 1985 is one of the best wines of the vintage–rich, supple, and meaty–and the 1989 is a massive wine of almost Californian intensity. Late picking of the grapes for the optimally ripe tannins is the general rule here, and the percentage of new oak *barriques* to mature the wine has been increased in recent years, though the exact percentage varies depending on the weight and style of the vintage. The superbly constituted 1996, for example, is being matured in 75 percent new oak.

Lynch-Bages in the 1990s is making claret well up to "super second growth" standard. The real caliber of a Bordeaux estate is always tested in off-vintages; in the rainy conditions of 1992 and 1993, Lynch-Bages produced wines of real fruit and substance resulting from rigorous selection of the best grapes. The 1994 for medium-term drinking (six to eight years) is a fine Cabernet-dominated wine and a "good buy" as Bordeaux prices sky-rocket. The 1995 and 1996 are great vintages to which old Jean-Charles would have doffed his hat.

> ## TASTING NOTES
>
> ### CHATEAU LYNCH-BAGES 1994
>
> Lustrous deep but elegant ruby; exceptional purity of Cabernet Sauvignon-led fruit on nose and palate; notes of cassis and cigar-box, typical high class Pauillac—very well made, the tannins silky.
> An exceptional 1994.
> Rating ★★★★

Jean-Michel Cazes, owner of Château Lynch-Bages.

CHATEAU MARGAUX

33460 Margaux, France
Tel: (33-5) 57 88 83 83 Fax: (33-5) 57 88 83 32
Visitors: by appointment

*C*hâteau Margaux emerged as one of the four great named clarets at the beginning of the eighteenth century, when it was drunk to acclaim in the coffeehouses of the City of London. Thomas Jefferson, on a visit to Bordeaux in 1787, chose Margaux as his favorite among "the four vineyards of quality" in preference to Lafite, Latour, and Haut-Brion. One must admire his taste, for two centuries on it is still the most

FACT BOX

OWNERS: Mentzelopoulos and Agnelli families

WINEMAKER: Paul Pontallier

SIZE OF VINEYARD: 195 acres

SECOND WINE: Pavillon Rouge de Château Margaux

TOTAL ANNUAL PRODUCTION: 31,000 cases

GRAPE VARIETIES: Cabernet Sauvignon 75 percent; Merlot 20 percent; Petit Verdot 3 percent; Cabernet Franc 2 percent

AVERAGE AGE OF VINES: 30 years

PERCENTAGE OF NEW WOOD: 100 percent

BEST RECENT VINTAGES: 1996, 1990, 1988, 1986, 1983, 1982, 1978

BEST DISHES TO MATCH WINES: simple roasts and grills of beef, and lamb

LOCAL RESTAURANTS: Relais de Margaux, Le Savoie, Margaux

refined and subtly generous of all clarets. And the château itself, built in the colonnaded style of the First Empire, is unquestionably the grandest piece of architecture in the Médoc.

With the acquisition of the estate in 1977 by the late André Mentzelopoulos of the Felix Potin grocery chain, Château Margaux entered one of the most brilliant periods in its history. Vast sums were invested in the vineyards, *chai*, and château. The 1978 is a very great wine, superbly rich and long-flavored, that will drink well into the next century. Sadly, Mentzelopoulos died suddenly in 1980 before he could enjoy the fruits of his investment, but in his attractive and very astute daughter, Corinne, now president of the enterprise, he had the best possible successor. Under her assured leadership and the technical direction of Paul

Pontallier, a sequence of remarkable wines were made in 1982, 1983, 1986, 1988 (the dark horse), 1990, and 1996. The 1994 is a graceful, very *Margollais* claret for medium-term drinking. The increased planting of Cabernet Sauvignon since 1978 has added a structure to the wines, which was sometimes lacking in the 1960s and 1970s. Pavillon Rouge, Château Margaux's second wine, compares in quality, (and less congenially in price), with some Médoc Second Growths.

ROBERT MONDAVI

7801 St. Helena Highway, P.O. Box 106,
Oakville, California 94562, USA
Tel: (707) 259 9463
*Visitors: daily, May–October 9:00AM–5:00PM,
November–April 9:30AM–4:30PM*

*R*obert Mondavi is America's best-known vintner. A tirelessly innovative winemaker and the father of Californian wine as we know it today, Mondavi communicates the pleasure of drinking good wine like nobody else, and he has been a great defender of the wine industry against the attacks of the new prohibitionists in the U.S.

Mondavi's Cabernet Sauvignon Reserve is the wine on which he has based his reputation. Three-quarters of the grapes for this classic Cabernet are grown in the choicest sites of central Napa Valley,

FACT BOX

OWNER: Robert Mondavi
WINEMAKER: Tim Mondavi
SIZE OF VINEYARD: 250 acres
TOTAL ANNUAL PRODUCTION:
35,000 cases
GRAPE VARIETY: Cabernet Sauvignon
AVERAGE AGE OF VINES: 30 years
PERCENTAGE OF NEW WOOD:
71 percent
BEST RECENT VINTAGES: 1996, 1995,
1994, 1992, 1991, 1990
BEST DISHES TO MATCH WINES:
rack of lamb, rare roast beef
LOCAL RESTAURANTS: Mustards,
Yountville Diner, Yountville

including Mondavi's own To-Kalon vineyard surrounding his futuristic winery in Oakville. The wine has gone through many stylistic changes since the first vintage in 1965. The 1974 was a magnificent, hugely tannic wine. The vintages of the 1980s in general seemed less flamboyant, but with the classic 1992, we are back to the old style of the 1974 but with more immediacy of pure fruit flavors. The tannins are softer due to gentler handling of the grapes and longer vatting times of up to 27 days.

Of all Mondavi's wine initiatives, it is his joint venture with the late Baron Philippe de Rothschild in creating a new wine, called Opus One, that has caused the greatest stir.

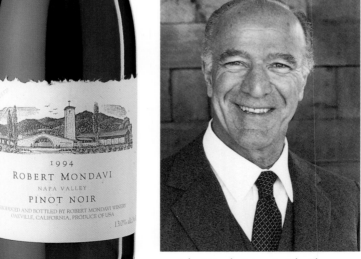

Robert Mondavi, America's best-known vintner.

Mondavi's futuristic winery in Oakville,
California.

Since the first vintage in 1979, the aim has been to produce a
Cabernet-based wine that combines the voluptuous appeal of Napa
with the structured class of a great Médoc. Early vintages were
judged over-oaked, but since 1985 the wine has begun to show
a balance and subtle power that
meets the goals of the partners. Most
recently, the Opus vintages of 1987,
1991, 1994, and 1996 have been
conspicuously successful.

TASTING NOTES

ROBERT MONDAVI CABERNET SAUVIGNON RESERVE 1992

Classic aromas of
blackcurrant; multilayered
flavors of black fruits and
berries enhanced with the
vanilla tones of new Nevers
French oak; excellent structure
and elegant definition of
flavor. A wine that will reach
its peak around 1999 to
2002. Rating ★★★★

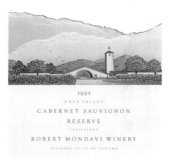

1992
NAPA VALLEY
CABERNET SAUVIGNON
RESERVE
UNFILTERED
ROBERT MONDAVI WINERY
ALCOHOL 13.5% BY VOLUME

CHATEAU MOUTON-ROTHSCHILD

33250 Pauillac, France
Tel: (33-5) 56 59 22 22 Fax: (33-5) 56 73 20 44
Visitors: welcome at wine museum during opening hours

*I*n many ways the most dramatic and theatrical of Bordeaux wine châteaux, Mouton is the lifetime's achievement of the late Baron Philippe de Rothschild, who died in 1988. Polymath, poet, theatrical impressario, and ocean-racing yachtsman, he was a man of rigorous intellect, freewheeling imagination, and almost limitless energy. Everything he set his hand to became something special, and the wine estate that he inherited in 1923 at the age of 21 was no exception.

FACT BOX

OWNER: Baronne Philippine de Rothschild

WINEMAKER: Patrick Leon

SIZE OF VINEYARD: 200 acres

TOTAL ANNUAL PRODUCTION: 33,000 cases

GRAPE VARIETIES: Cabernet Sauvignon 78 percent; Cabernet Franc 10 percent; Merlot 10 percent; Petit Verdot 2 percent

AVERAGE AGE OF VINES: 45 years

PERCENTAGE OF NEW WOOD: 80–100 percent depending on vintage

BEST RECENT VINTAGES: 1996, 1986

BEST DISHES TO MATCH WINES: Venison, saddle of lamb, sirloin of beef

LOCAL RESTAURANT: Château Cordeillan-Bages, Pauillac

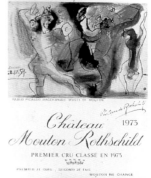

Château Mouton-Rothschild in Pauillac.

In 1925, Rothschild decided that all his wine should be bottled at the château rather than in Bordeaux, a revolutionary notion at the time. And after World War II, he came up with the inspired idea of commissioning each year a different, often world-famous, artist to paint a picture for the upper part of the label. The work of such artists as Chagall and Andy Warhol have adorned every vintage of Mouton since 1945. As a belated recognition of the wine's stature, in 1973 the château was promoted to First Growth status. The estate is now owned by Philippe's only child, Philippine, a woman of charm and theatrical flair, who has continued her father's joint venture with the Mondavi family in California at Opus One (*qv*). Her latest wine project in Chile started production in 1997.

The soil of the Mouton-Rothschild vineyard is largely gravel and flint, which explains why a high proportion of Cabernet Sauvignon (78 percent) is planted. Mouton is thus closer in style to Latour than to its neighbor, Lafite. On top form since the early 1980s, it is a Pauillac of balanced power and succulence. The 1982 is magnificent and great wines were made here in 1986 and 1996, quintessential Cabernet years.

> ## TASTING NOTES
>
> ### CHATEAU MOUTON-ROTHSCHILD 1994
>
> With the first picture by a Dutch artist, Karel Appel, on the label, this is a Mouton of power relieved by silky charm. Aromas of roasted coffee and black fruits, strong Cabernet character underpinned with fine tannins; lovely balance and first growth length. A top wine in a respectable year.
>
> **Rating ★★★★**

BODEGAS MUGA

Barrio de la Estacion, 26200 Haro, Spain
Tel: (941) 310825 Fax: (941) 312868
Visitors: Monday–Friday at 11:00AM

*T*he red wines from this outstanding family-run *bodegas* are everything great Rioja should be: rich, complex flavors, just the right amount of oak, a capacity to age magnificently. The wines at Reserva level are also terrific value for money, selling at under $15 a bottle retail.

The *bodegas* was founded in 1932 by Isaac Muga, the scion of an old family of Riojan growers. His son, Isaac Junior, has run the company since 1969 with a total commitment to the highest standards of quality. In 1971, the *bodegas* became a

FACT BOX

OWNER: Bodegas Muga S.A.

WINEMAKER: Muga family

SIZE OF VINEYARD: 112.5 acres

TOTAL ANNUAL PRODUCTION: 75,000 cases

GRAPE VARIETIES: Tempranillo 70 percent; and smaller amounts of Gamacha, Graciano, and Mazuelo

AVERAGE AGE OF VINES: 6 years

PERCENTAGE OF NEW WOOD: 10 percent (⅔ American oak, ⅓ French oak)

BEST RECENT VINTAGES: 1995, 1994, 1989, 1987, 1985

BEST BUY: 1994

BEST DISHES TO MATCH WINES: venison, red meats, strong cheeses

LOCAL RESTAURANTS: Beethoven, Terete, Atamauri (all in Haro)

corporation, but the family retained a majority of the shares, thus ensuring a continuity of the traditional, uncompromising style of Rioja production practiced by old Isaac. The whole process of making, storing, and aging the wines, for example, takes place in wood—very few rival houses can say the same.

The firm has good-sized vineyards in the best sites of the Rioja Alta, but buys in most of

> ### TASTING NOTES
> #### MUGA RESERVA 1994
>
> Superb deep-purple color with scarlet tints; strong impression of complexity on nose and palate; wonderful blackberry fruit and scents of roasted coffee overlay; latent mineral flavors that will develop with age. Drink 1999–2007.
> A great wine.
> Rating ★★★★

its grapes from about 40 small farmers, some of whom have been supplying Muga for three generations. "We believe in small farmers," says Isaac Junior, "because they have small surfaces and they pay a lot of attention to the grapes. They also know that we like the very best grapes and will pay the price."

Red winemaking and tending is a craft at Muga. The firm has its own cooperage, renewing and repairing about three barrels a day. Racking is performed by gravity, that is, through a hollow

Fermenting grapes in oak tanks.

cane from barrel to barrel, the aim being to eliminate impurities and oxygenate the wines. They are never filtered.

All this tender loving care shows in the glass. The 1989 Reserva was one of the all-time red wine bargains, great wells of blackberry fruit mingling with the creamy vanillin richness of the oak. If you can still find stock in a specialist merchant's catalogue, don't hesitate, for it will still be drinking splendidly at the new millenium and beyond. The

1994, released in Spring 1998, will be another outstanding wine (*see* Tasting Notes). The top-of-the-range Prado Enea Rioja Gran Reserva is undeniably a very great wine in both the 1987 and 1985 vintages but is extremely expensive. The straight Reservas are the best buys here.

The splendid dining room at Bodegas Muga.

CHATEAU PAPE CLEMENT

33600 Pessac, Bordeaux, France
Tel: (33-5) 56 07 04 11 Fax: (33-5) 56 07 36 70
*Visitors: by appointment, Monday–Friday 9:00AM–12 NOON
and 2:00PM–5:00PM*

*T*his vineyard was planted in 1300 by Archbishop Bernard de Hoth, the future Pope Clement V, and remained the property of the Church until the French Revolution. Since 1939 it has belonged to the family of the French poet, Paul Montagne. Although situated nowadays in the suburbs of Bordeaux, the vineyard extends across a wide plateau characterized by the lightness and complexity of the soil. There is sand, there is gravel, and also trace elements of iron.

FACT BOX

OWNERS: Montagne family

WINEMAKER: Bernard Pujol

SIZE OF VINEYARD: 75 acres

SECOND WINE: Le Clementin du Château Pape Clement

TOTAL ANNUAL PRODUCTION: 10,000 cases

GRAPE VARIETIES: Cabernet Sauvignon 60 percent; Merlot 40 percent

AVERAGE AGE OF VINES: 39 years

PERCENTAGE OF NEW WOOD: 80–90 percent

BEST RECENT VINTAGES: 1996, 1990

BEST DISHES TO MATCH WINES: beef, mushrooms

LOCAL RESTAURANT: Le Chapon Fin, Bordeaux

TASTING NOTES

CHATEAU PAPE CLEMENT 1995

Lovely purple ruby, deep but not overextracted; gorgeous aroma of spring flowers (young Merlot to the fore) and a subtle hint of vanilla from the oak; deceptively forward but with great balance and superfine tannins. Class in a glass.
Rating ★★★★

This *terroir* and the classic 60/40 mix of Cabernet Sauvignon and Merlot shape a wine of elegant and beautifully defined flavors. Following a sequence of thin and dilute wines in the 1970s and early 1980s, a new winemaker, Bernard Pujol, was appointed in 1985. Since then, Pape-Clement has returned to top form, the wines showing the distinctive tobacco aromas and supple, opulent texture of old. The winemaking is essentially classical with intelligent modern touches. For example, the malolactic fermentation, the process that makes wine softer and rounder, is conducted half in *barriques*, half in stainless steel in order to avoid too woody a flavor in the finished wine. Yet Pujol is a believer in new oak, having increased the proportion to 80 or 90 percent in good vintages. He obviously has a very light touch, for the wines never taste over-

oaked. Splendidly deep-flavored yet balanced wines were made in 1986, 1988, and 1990. The 1995 is a fragrant charmer; the 1996 has the stuff of greatness and is pervaded with the taste of especially ripe Cabernet Sauvignon.

PENFOLD'S GRANGE

Tanunda Road, Nuriootpa, Barossa, South Australia
Visitors: not open to the public

*T*he birth of Grange, Australia's preeminent red wine, was painful and protracted. In 1950, Max Schubert, Penfold's chief winemaker, made an extensive tour of the Bordeaux vineyards and returned to the Barossa fired with the ambition to make an Australian red wine, with a complexity and capacity to age, comparable to a great claret or Rhône.

Schubert made an experimental five barrels of red wine from Shiraz grapes in 1951, repeated the same formula in 1952, then made a third experimental wine from 100 percent Cabernet Sauvignon for the 1953 vintage. But when his bosses at

FACT BOX

OWNERS: Southcorp Wines

WINEMAKER: John Duval

SIZE OF VINEYARD: grapes come from several sources

TOTAL ANNUAL PRODUCTION: 5,000–10,000 cases, depending on vintage

GRAPE VARIETY: up to 99 percent Shiraz

AVERAGE AGE OF VINES: not specified

PERCENTAGE OF NEW WOOD: 100 percent American oak

BEST RECENT VINTAGES: 1990

BEST DISHES TO MATCH WINES: venison, game, roast and grilled meats

Penfolds tasted the black tannic wines, they were horrified. Declaring the wines to be no better than dry ports, they promptly ordered Schubert to stop production of Grange immediately. Fortunately, like all great winemakers, Schubert was a little obsessive and quietly continued to make Grange under cover, with the tacit approval of his loyal staff. In 1960, the Penfolds directors were persuaded to retaste the early

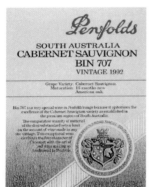

wines, which by then had started to shed their tannins to reveal extraordinary richness of fruit and depth of flavor. Schubert was given the go-ahead and the finance to make Grange into one of the world's best red wines.

Unlike its great rival, Henschke's Hill of Grace, Grange does not draw its fruit from a single vineyard but from various sources in Barossa, the Southern Vales, and even, it has been suggested, from Padthaway and the Hunter Valley on occasions. Fermentation is conducted at warm temperatures in stainless steel. The wine is then drawn off and lodged in new American oak casks for 18 months to achieve a good balance of fruit and oxygenated complexity, very much the

Grange style. Shiraz completely dominates the grape mix, though between one and 13 percent Cabernet Sauvignon may be added, depending on the vintage.

CHATEAU PETRUS

33500 Pomerol, France
Tel: (33-5) 57 51 78 96 Fax: (33-5) 57 51 79 79
Visitors: strictly by appointment

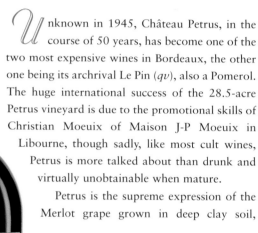

$\mathcal{U}$nknown in 1945, Château Petrus, in the course of 50 years, has become one of the two most expensive wines in Bordeaux, the other one being its archrival Le Pin (*qv*), also a Pomerol. The huge international success of the 28.5-acre Petrus vineyard is due to the promotional skills of Christian Moeuix of Maison J-P Moeuix in Libourne, though sadly, like most cult wines, Petrus is more talked about than drunk and virtually unobtainable when mature.

Petrus is the supreme expression of the Merlot grape grown in deep clay soil,

FACT BOX

OWNERS: Lacoste, Loubet, and Moeuix families

WINEMAKER: Christian Moeuix

SIZE OF VINEYARD: 28.5 acres

TOTAL ANNUAL PRODUCTION: 4,500 cases

GRAPE VARIETIES: Merlot 95 percent; Cabernet Franc 5 percent

AVERAGE AGE OF VINES: 40 years

PERCENTAGE OF NEW WOOD: up to 100 percent

BEST RECENT VINTAGES: 1995, 1990, 1989, 1986, 1985, 1982

BEST DISHES TO MATCH WINES: game, mushrooms, spicy oriental duck

LOCAL HOTEL/RESTAURANT: Hostellerie Plaisance, St. Emilion

TASTING NOTES

CHATEAU PETRUS 1994

Dramatic black-cherry color, voluptuous bouquet of Asian spices and raspberries (easy to confuse with great Burgundy); beautiful mouthfeel, like velvet, but with a firm, classic underpinning of ripe tannins and the potential to develop lovely nuances of flavor. Drink from 2003. A superb 1994.
Rating ★★★★

where it thrives. The wine is extremely rich and concentrated. This is due to the good age of the vines (averaging 40 years) and especially to the policy of keeping the yields of wine as restricted as possible. Exceptional wines were made in 1945, 1947, 1949, 1950, 1953, 1961, 1967 and, controversially, 1971, a track record confirmed by a string of astounding successes in the 1970s. As the vines have gotten older, so the style of the later wines have become increasingly monumental, heady, and slow-maturing. The 1982 and 1985 are magnificent and are just beginning to drink well; the 1986 is hugely tannic and should not be touched for 20 years; the 1989 is more flattering, almost Californian in its unctuous intensity; the 1994 is perhaps the best wine of the year on Bordeaux's right bank.

Hard though it is to find a bottle, explore every avenue that leads you to the chance of tasting Petrus, young or old. It is one of the great organoleptic experiences.

CHATEAU PICHON LONGUEVILLE COMTESSE DE LALANDE

33250 Pauillac, France
Tel: (33-5) 56 59 19 40 Fax: (33-5) 56 59 26 56
Visitors: by appointment

*I*n contrast to Pichon Baron, its arch rival across the road, Pichon Comtesse is an elegant 1840s mansion. The gracious but iron-willed May-Elaine de Lencquesaing, Comtesse's hands-on owner since 1978, is the driving force behind the renaissance of a wine now rated as one of the very finest in Pauillac and the equal of the First Growths. No surprise really, for the vineyards of Comtesse

FACT BOX

OWNER: May-Elaine de Lencquesaing
WINEMAKER: Thomas Do Chi Nam
SIZE OF VINEYARD: 188.75 acres
SECOND WINE: Reserve de Comtesse
TOTAL ANNUAL PRODUCTION: 30,000 cases
GRAPE VARIETIES: Cabernet Sauvignon 45 percent; Merlot 34 percent; Cabernet Franc 13 percent; Petit Verdot 8 percent
AVERAGE AGE OF VINES: 25 years
PERCENTAGE OF NEW WOOD: up to 70 percent
BEST RECENT VINTAGES: 1996, 1989, 1990, 1989
BEST DISHES TO MATCH WINES: roast grouse and woodcock, navarin of lamb
LOCAL RESTAURANT: Château Cordeillan Bages, Pauillac

of Comtesse lie next door to those of Latour, but with the significant difference that a third of them are located in the *appellation* of St. Julien, these vines bringing a suppleness and floral elegance to the wine which is all its own. Darkly colored, rich and fruity, it is a rare instance of a great Médoc that has more than 30 percent Merlot in the blend.

Madame de Lencquesaing's reforming zeal has resulted in an extended *chai*, a new winery, and much improved facilities both for tasting and receiving guests, as well as a complete renovation of the charming château and park. Under her firm leadership, Pichon Comtesse has had a better track record of brilliant vintages in the last 20 years than any other Bordeaux château. So anyone farsighted enough to have stashed away the great vintages of the 1980s–especially the 1989, 1986, and 1982–can look forward to some spectacular drinking in the next few years. *Bravo, Madame.*

The elegant 1840s mansion belonging to
Pichon Comtesse.

RIDGE VINEYARDS

17100 Monte Bello Road, P.O. Box 1810,
Cupertino, California 95015, USA
Tel: (408) 867-3244 Fax: (408) 867-2986
*Visitors: Monte Bello (Cupertino), all year,
Saturday and Sunday 11:00AM–3:00PM*

*R*idge Cabernets and Zinfandels regularly feature among the top wines of a California vintage, true classics in the sense that they can compete with the best in the world. To understand fully the greatness of Ridge, it helps to look closely at the way in which the wines are made and their originating vineyards.

Although born into the new age of technological California wine in the early 1960s, Ridge had a fundamentally different approach to winemaking from most other makers. As Paul Draper, the winemaker and driving force at the estates

TASTING NOTES

RIDGE MONTEBELLO 1993

Intense near-opaque purple ruby; still closed, with a classic austerity on the nose but the promise of rich black fruits and licorice to come; monumental and concentrated on the palate but with a fine raciness, tension and lovely balance. This is a true classic and one to keep until 2003/2005. Last tasted January 1998.

Rating ★★★★★

since 1969, puts it: "Our approach is straightforward: find the most intense and flavorful grapes, intrude minimally on the natural process, draw all the fruit's richness into the wine."

Great wines depend, of course, on great grapes grown in an exceptional place. At Montebello Ridge up in the Santa Cruz mountains south of San Francisco Bay, the first vintages convinced the founding partners that here was a perfect site with an astonishing match of climate, soil, and varietal. Having identified a great vineyard, a rare achievement in the wine world, the partners then did everything they could to gain full, long-term control if it in order to maintain quality and

RIDGE 1993
CALIFORNIA
MONTE BELLO®

86% CABERNET IN A VINEYARD BLEND
GROWN, PRODUCED & BOTTLED BY RIDGE VINEYARDS
17100 MONTE BELLO ROAD, CUPERTINO, CALIFORNIA
12.5% VOL.   PRODUCE OF U.S.A.   1500 ML

RIDGE 1995
CALIFORNIA
LYTTON SPRINGS®

84% ZINFANDEL IN A VINEYARD BLEND
PRODUCED AND BOTTLED BY RIDGE VINEYARDS   BW 4488
17100 MONTE BELLO ROAD, BOX 1810, CUPERTINO, CA 95014
14.5% VOL.   PRODUCE OF CALIFORNIA U.S.A.   750 ML

FACT BOX

OWNER: Mr. Akihisto Otsuka

WINEMAKER: Paul Draper

SIZE OF VINEYARD: Monte Bello Estate—131 acres; Lytton Springs Estate—157 acres; Geyserville Vineyard—85 acres

TOTAL ANNUAL PRODUCTION: 65,000 cases

GRAPE VARIETIES: Monte Bello—Cabernet Sauvignon 57.4 percent; Merlot 20.2 percent; Chardonnay 15.3 percent; Zinfandel 4.6 percent; Petit Verdot 1.5 percent; Cabernet Franc 1.0 percent

Lytton Springs—Zinfandel 71.1 percent; Petite Sirah 11.3 percent; Grenache 5.9 percent; Syrah 5.9 percent; Barbera 2.7 percent; Mataro 2.6 percent; Carignan 0.5 percent

Geyserville Vineyard—Zinfandel 65 percent; Carignan 20 percent; Petite Sirah 15 percent

AVERAGE AGE OF VINES: Montebello Estate—30 years; Lytton Springs Estate—50 years; Geyserville Vineyard—60 years

PERCENTAGE OF NEW WOOD: 100 percent for Cabernets, 20 percent for Zinfandels; all in air-dried American oak

BEST RECENT VINTAGES: 1991, 1992, 1994, 1995, 1996

BEST BUY: 1993

BEST DISHES TO MATCH WINES: southwestern lamb stew with Cabernets; venison burger with *chèvre* and a spicy tomato relish with Zinfandels

LOCAL RESTAURANTS AND HOTELS: Sent Sovi, Saratoga; Stanford Court Hotel, Palo Alto

consistency. Montebello–with its cool location 15 miles from the Pacific Ocean, mature vines, and well-drained limestone subsoils–continues to produce some of the most distinctive Cabernet and Merlot in California. Ridge now owns or leases all its vineyards on Montebello Ridge. Across the bay in Sonoma, over 30 vintages from Geyserville's old-vine Zinfandel, Carignan, and Petit Syrah are striking evidence of another astounding combination of location and varietals. At the nearby Lytton Springs vineyard, 20 years of experience has convinced Draper that it, is an exceptional site.

Paul Draper, Winemaker.

In the vineyards, the yields of grape juice per vine are low; in the case of Montebello, often half that of estates in Napa or, indeed, in Bordeaux. Paul Draper is a practical winemaker. With a wry smile he says, "we harvest more by taste than by sugar and acid numbers." Yet he and his original partners have always asked themselves the hard analytical question: why is it that better wine is made by traditional methods? Their answer is that minimal treatment in the winery (for example, no filtration) gives to the wine a rich vinosity that carries the high tannins along to an eventually splendid maturity.

In great vintages Monte Bello, a classic blend of Cabernet Sauvignon and Merlot with smaller additions of Petit Verdot and Cabernet Franc, will be alive and vigorous after 25 years; the 1962, one of Draper's favorite vintages, is still showing well. The vintages of the 1990s have provided the longest run of top wines in Ridge's 35-year history. The 1996, tasted as a cask sample in London in June 1997, may be the greatest of all. Customers wanting a taste of the greatness of Ridge at reasonable cost should opt for the Bridgehead Mataro (Mourvedre); the 1995 brims with juicy fruit made more complex by notes of leather and pepper–a great steak wine.

SAN GUIDO SASSICAIA

Tenuta San Guido, 57020 Bolgheri (Livorno), Italy
Tel: (39-565) 76 20 03 Fax: (39-565) 76 20 17
Visitors: by appointment

*S*assicaia was the first of the *barrique*-aged Super Tuscans. This internationally acclaimed wine was created in the early 1940s by Marchese Mario Incisa della Rocchetta from the Cabernet Sauvignon and Cabernet Franc vines he planted on his estate at Bolgheri, near Livorno on the Mediterranean coast. For over 20 years the wine was consumed only privately. Then, in 1968, it was offered to the market. Incisa's revolutionary choice of grape, the seaside location of the vineyard, and his vinification methods quickly caught the imagination of the wine world, especially in

FACT BOX

OWNER: Marchese Nicolo Incisa della Rochetta

WINEMAKER: Incisa family

SIZE OF VINEYARD: 125 acres

TOTAL ANNUAL PRODUCTION: 10,000 cases

GRAPE VARIETIES: Cabernet Sauvignon 85 percent; Cabernet Franc 15 percent

AVERAGE AGE OF VINES: 30 years

PERCENTAGE OF NEW WOOD: 40 percent

BEST RECENT VINTAGES: 1995, 1990, 1985

BEST DISHES TO MATCH WINES: *cinghali* (wild boar stew)

LOCAL RESTAURANT: Enoteca, Florence

America. By the 1980s Sassicaia was a cult wine in the fashionable restaurants of New York, Los Angeles, and San Franciso and priced accordingly. It is usually an exceptional bottle that regularly upstages prestigious First-Growth St.-Emilions at blind tastings.

Sassicaia is a blend of 85 percent Cabernet Sauvignon and 15 percent Cabernet Franc grown on very stony soils that yield low quantities of fruit, significantly less than those of many Bordeaux chateaux. Vinification takes

> ## TASTING NOTES
> ### SASSICAIA 1994
> Deep brooding ruby with purple highlights suggesting very concentrated wine. Just so. Densely fruity, with hints of the herbs of the Maremmo; strongly tannic, very powerful, Cabernet-dominated palate, uncompromising and needing 20 years to reach maturity. Last tasted January 1998.
> Rating ★★★

place in stainless steel, followed by 24 months of *barrique* aging. The wine is then rested for 12–16 months before release.

Generally speaking, Sassicaia reaches its peak for optimum drinking in 8–12 years. At full maturity, the wine has an intense bouquet of Morello cherries and wild herbs; the balance of fruit and oak is excellent. There is a fragrance to the flavor that speaks class and refinement, and the finish is long and velvety. In recent years, the two greatest vintages have been 1985 and 1990. Sassicaia was promoted from Super Tuscan *vino da tavola* to Bolgheri DOC in 1994.

Agronomist Alessandro Petri in the vineyards at Sassicaia.

SILVER OAK CELLARS

P.O. Box 141, Oakville, California 94562, USA
Tel: (1-707) 944 8808 Fax: (1-707) 944 2817
Visitors: by appointment only

*F*or sheer hedonistic pleasure, the Cabernet Sauvignons of Silver Oak are in a class of their own. Ever since Justin Meyer founded the estate near the Oakville crossroads of central Napa Valley in 1972, he has always wanted to produce voluptuous rich wines that would give immediate satisfaction on release without compromising their ability to age. So it does not come as a surprise to learn that two-thirds of Silver Oak's production is sold within California, or that 60 percent of total output is earmarked for fashionable restaurants across America.

Although based in Napa, the majority of Silver Oaks' vineyards (some 200 acres)

FACT BOX

OWNERS: Justin and Bonny Meyer
WINEMAKER: Justin Meyer
SIZE OF VINEYARD: 238 acres
TOTAL ANNUAL PRODUCTION:
40,000 cases
GRAPE VARIETY: Cabernet Sauvignon
AVERAGE AGE OF VINES: 25 years
PERCENTAGE OF NEW WOOD:
50 percent (Alexander Valley),
100 percent (Napa Valley)
BEST RECENT VINTAGES: 1996, 1994,
1992, 1991, 1990
BEST DISHES TO MATCH WINES:
venison and all red meats
LOCAL RESTAURANT: Domaine
Chandon, Napa

are in the old North Coast district of Alexander Valley. A further 38 acres in Napa include the tiny, single "Bonny's" vineyard across from the winery. All three wines are made from 100 percent Cabernet Sauvignon. The wonder is that without the softening effect of Merlot, they are never overharsh or greenly tannic. Justin believes that this is due to the super ripeness of the late-picked grapes, the mineral richness of the soils, and the Kentucky and Missouri origins of the American oak barrels in which the wines pass a lengthy spell of up to 30 months.

Although the three wines share a lavish style, each is very individual. In simple terms, the Alexander Valley is ready soonest, with soft black-fruits flavors and a well-judged, naturally sweet note of American oak.

> ### TASTING NOTES
>
> #### SILVER OAK CABERNET SAUVIGNON ALEXANDER VALLEY 1990
>
> Even, deep lustrous ruby; vibrant bouquet of blackcurrants and cherries; silky texture in the mouth, the sumptuous fruit mingling with secondary vinous flavors and the discreet sweetness of the oak. Round and smooth but in no way overblown. Ace.
> Rating ★★★★

The Napa is more elegant, but with a durable structure to ensure a long life. The Bonny's Vineyard is massively concentrated, but as its production has been so tiny, from the 1993 vintage onward the label is being phased out, the wine going into the Napa Cuvée. If there are any lingering doubts about the aging potential of such seductive wines, the 1974 Silver Oak Napa Cuvée is still full of life and fruit at a time when so many California Cabernets of that fabled vintage are now dead in the glass. The 1990 Silver Oak wines, both the Alexander Valley and the Napa Cuvée, will be drinking perfectly for the new millenium; the 1992s, 1994s, and 1996s are real keepers that should be stashed away for a deliriously happy old age.

SILVER OAK®
1983
NAPA VALLEY
Cabernet Sauvignon
Cellared and bottled by SILVER OAK CELLARS
Oakville, Napa County, California
Alcohol 13.1% by Volume

BODEGAS VEGA SICILIA

*T*he most traditional and famous wine estate in Spain, Vega Sicilia produces the country's greatest and longest-lived red wines. Don Eloy Lecanda, a rich Basque landowner, founded the *bodegas* in 1864, and immediately ordered from a Bordeaux nurseryman vine stock of Cabernet Sauvignon, Merlot, and Malbec to complement the local Ribera Tempranillo and Albillo already planted in the vineyard. There are currently 400 acres under vine, producing around 17,000 cases, though the Alvarez family, who have owned the

FACT BOX

OWNER: Pablo Alvarez

WINEMAKER: Alvarez family

SIZE OF VINEYARD: 400 acres

TOTAL ANNUAL PRODUCTION:
17,000 cases

GRAPE VARIETIES: Ribera Tempranillo
65 percent; Cabernet Sauvignon 15
percent; remainder Malbec and Albillo

AVERAGE AGE OF VINES: 35 years

PERCENTAGE OF NEW WOOD:
none (old casks)

BEST RECENT VINTAGES: 1994,
1987, 1976

BEST DISHES TO MATCH WINES:
wine-based casseroles of game, beef,
or pork

TASTING NOTES

VEGA SICILIA GRAN RESERVA 1976

Still youthful, deep ruby color, wonderful depth of black-cherry fruit on nose and palate; fleshy, mouthfilling, velvety texture, the flavor going on and on. Top-flight.
Rating ★★★★★

estate since 1962, plan to increase the production gradually to 25,000 cases. Vine tending and winemaking remain rigorously classical; yields are low, and the wines spend a long time in cask before bottling.

From the range, the Valbuena "fifth year" reserva offers the best value for money – a garnet cherry red with brick-hued reflections, a ripe black-fruits aroma, and an excellent balance of primary fruit, vinosity, and oak on the palate. The vintage Vega Sicilia Unico Gran Reservas are the wines on which the *bodegas*' awesome reputation is based. Never released before they are 10 years old and normally not reaching their peak for 20 or even 30 years, these wines, though clearly marked by the oxygenating effects of oak, retain a remarkably vigorous flavor of pure fruit into their old age. The 1976 (*see* Tasting Notes) is excellent; both the 1970, scented and voluptuous, and the 1968, massive and concentrated, are magnificent. Top-of-the-range Vega Unico Special Reserva is a blend of very old wines from the 1950s and 1960s and ruinously priced; I have never tasted a bottle, which is hardly surprising as nearly all this wine is stashed away in the private cellars of very rich Spaniards.

THE RED WINE *directory*

BENCHMARKERS

BAVA

Strada Monferrato 2, 14023 Coconato d'Asti, Piedmont, Italy
Tel: (39-141) 90 70 83 Fax: (39-141) 90 70 85
*Visitors: Monday–Friday 8:00AM–12:00 NOON and
2:00PM–6:00PM; Saturdays 8:00AM–12:00 NOON*

*T*he tight-knit Bava family work out of a traditional winery next to the railway station in the delightful hilltop village of Cocconato. Tucked between Asti and the Alps, this is the Monferrato district of Piedmont and home to Barbera, the other great red wine grape of northwest Italy. This splendid variety, suffused with an almost fruitcake richness, used to stand in the shadow of Nebbiolo, the famous grape that makes Barolo. But in the early 1980s, Bava was one of the few companies pioneering new-style world-

FACT BOX

OWNERS: Bava family

WINEMAKER: Paolo Bava

SIZE OF VINEYARD: 250 acres

TOTAL ANNUAL PRODUCTION:
50,000–80,000 cases

GRAPE VARIETIES: Barbera, Nebbiolo, Dolcetto, Malvasia Nero, Rucche

AVERAGE AGE OF VINES: 20 years

PERCENTAGE OF NEW WOOD:
100 percent for new-generation wines; well-aged Slovenian oak for Barolo

BEST RECENT VINTAGES: 1994, 1993, 1991

BEST DISHES TO MATCH WINES:
fritto misto, white truffles, seasoned cheeses

LOCAL RESTAURANT: Ristorante Cannon d'Oro, Cocconato

Bava's vineyards in Cocconato, Piedmont.

class wines made from 100 percent Barbera aged in *barriques*. Bringing the individual flavors of Piedmont's native grapes to a wider world is a mission for the Bava family. Natural marketeers as well as serious winemakers, they put on classical and jazz concerts in the village, which are just the thing after a huge plate of *fritto misto* at the excellent Ristorante Cannon d'Oro in the main piazza.

Stradivario, the firm's flagship Barbera, is instantly recognizable from its violin motif on the label, and comes from grapes grown in the Cocconato vineyard of Gura. It is aged in new Allier French oak for 12 months and spends another year in bottle before release. The new oak presence is noticeable at first, but melds into the wine after a good period of ageing. For those who like a less obviously

TASTING NOTES

STRADIVARIO COLLEZIONE QUINTETTO BAVA 1994

Youthful color, deep ruby at center of the bowl. Toasty new oak on the nose melds with ripe black-cherry, spicy fruit. Quite concentrated, a fleshy full wine.

Rating ★★★

woody wine, Bava has introduced a Barbera called Arbest in a more traditional style. The main difference is that the Arbest is part-aged in large old casks. The company also produces a very elegant Barolo and delicious reds and rosés made from local varieties such as Ruche and Malvasia. If you are tired of the international flavor style of Cabernet Sauvignon, do try these lovely individual wines.

Bava's Barbera d'Asti.

DOMAINES BUNAN BANDOL

B.P. 17, 83740 La Cadière, France
Tel: (33-4) 94 98 58 98 Fax: (33-4) 94 98 60 05
Visitors: daily 8:00AM–12 NOON and 2:00PM–7:00PM
(closed Sunday in winter)

High above La Cadière d'Azur in spectacularly beautiful wine country lies the Moulin des Costes, headquarters of the charming and hospitable Paul and Pierre Bunan, makers of exemplary Bandol, one of the best red wines of France. Born Sephardic Jews in Algeria, the Bunans were forced to leave North Africa in 1960, so they came to the French Riviera and bought the Moulin and 45-acre vineyard a year later. The dynamic brothers have since acquired the 52.5-acre Château de la

FACT BOX

OWNERS: Bunan family

WINEMAKER: Paul, Pierre, and Laurent Bunan

SIZE OF VINEYARD: 200 acres

TOTAL ANNUAL PRODUCTION: 35,000 cases

GRAPE VARIETIES: Mourvedre 70 percent; Grenache 30 percent

AVERAGE AGE OF VINES: 50 years (Château de la Rouvière); 35 years (Moulin des Costes)

PERCENTAGE OF NEW WOOD: none (large, used, oak tuns preferred)

BEST RECENT VINTAGES: 1996, 1995, 1993

BEST DISHES TO MATCH WINES: grilled bream or red mullet (for red)

LOCAL RESTAURANTS: Le Relais de Mougins at Vence, Martinez at Cannes

Rouvière and a third property, the Domaine de Belouve, which they farm for the owner on a rental basis. Laurent Bunan, Paul's son, who studied at the Lycée Viticole in Beaune, now works full time at the *domaines*.

The red wine of Moulin des Costes is a strong but supple and finely made Bandol (70 percent Mourvedre, 30 percent Grenache) and there is an excellent rosé, too. The star of the range is the special *cuvée*, which only appears in outstanding vintages (1996, 1995, 1993) under the Château de la Rouvière label. Made exclusively from low-yielding, 50-year-old Mourvedre vines and aged in large, well-used oak tuns for 24 months, this is a big, heartwarming wine that deserves to be put away for 10 years and drunk with a loved one on a cold winter night.

TASTING NOTES

CHATEAU DE LA ROUVIERE 1993

Deep, dense, but lustrous ruby/purple; powerful vinous nose with hints of provençal herbs; on the palate an uncompromising wine, strong mordant tannins are the predominant impression, but if aged until 2003 will provide a spectacular bottle for game. Last tasted November 1997.

Rating ★★★★

CUVAISON

4550 Silverado Trail, P.O. Box 384, Calistoga,
California 94515, USA
Tel: (1-707) 942 6266 Fax: (1-707) 942 5732
Visitors: daily 10:00AM–5:00PM (except major holidays)

*S*ituated on the Silverado Trail in northern Napa Valley, Cuvaison has been on a steadily improving curve since John Thacher became chief winemaker in 1982. The strongest card here is the winery's exceptional 289-acre vineyard in the cool Carneros district, which John has played with consummate skill. "My style is to express the unique character of our estate grapes by doing as little as possible to them. With such wonderful fruit to work with, that should be one's emphasis."

FACT BOX

OWNERS: Schmidheiny family

WINEMAKER: John Thacher

SIZE OF VINEYARD: 289 acres

TOTAL ANNUAL PRODUCTION: 60,000 cases

GRAPE VARIETIES: Chardonnay 70 percent; Merlot 20 percent; Pinot Noir 10 percent

AVERAGE AGE OF VINES: 6 years

PERCENTAGE OF NEW WOOD: 50–70 percent

BEST RECENT VINTAGE: 1995

BEST DISHES TO MATCH WINES: pork tenderloin, rack of lamb, and swordfish

LOCAL RESTAURANT: Tra Vigne in Calistoga

About 70 percent of the vineyard is planted with Chardonnay, which sources an excellent barrel-fermented wine. There's a very good Merlot, too. But the real jewels here are the two Pinot Noirs on which John lavishes a lot of tender loving care. He ferments the wines in small stainless-steel tanks in order to control them better, and he doesn't fine them for fear of removing their aromatic pot-ential and nuances of flavor. The Carneros is sensuous, full but well-balanced, the aroma of tar smoke and vanilla leading on to rich berry-fruit flavors of some complexity. The Eris is more subtle, less oaky, just mouthwateringly delicious and a solace with or without food at any time of the day or night.

TASTING NOTES

CUVAISON ERIS PINOT NOIR 1995

Rich, ruby Pinot color; judicious new oak on nose, but finesse and delicacy are the keynotes; nuances of wild strawberries and redcurrants spiced with vanilla. Supple and silky; one of the best American Pinot Noirs.

Rating ★★★★

CHATEAU D'ANGLUDET

33460 Margaux, France
Tel: (33-5) 57 88 71 41 Fax: (33-5) 57 88 72 52
Visitors: by appointment only

*T*he vineyard of Château d'Angludet lies in the extreme southwestern corner of the Margaux *appellation* on a plateau of gravel called Le Grand Poujeaux. It is this soil that gives the wine its sturdy character and prospect of a long life. The house, a comfortable old farmhouse with a delightful duck pond, was the home of Peter A. Sichel, broker, President of the Union des Grands Crus, until his death in 1998. Peter and his fiancée, Diana Heathcote-Amory, bought the property in a dilapidated state in 1961 and raised a family of six children there. His sons, Charles and Benjamin, are now

FACT BOX

OWNER: Peter A. Sichel
WINEMAKER: Benjamin Sichel
SIZE OF VINEYARD: 87.5 acres
TOTAL ANNUAL PRODUCTION: 10,500 cases
GRAPE VARIETIES: Cabernet Sauvignon 55 percent; Merlot 35 percent; Cabernet Franc 5 percent; Petit Verdot 5 percent
AVERAGE AGE OF VINES: 28 years
PERCENTAGE OF NEW WOOD: 35–50 percent, depending on year
BEST RECENT VINTAGES: 1996, 1995
BEST BUY: 1994
BEST DISHES TO MATCH WINES: grilled meats, red or white, *Lamproie à la Bordelaise*
LOCAL RESTAURANTS: Le Pavillon de Margaux, Le Lion d'Or, Arcins

manager and winemaker of the estate, respectively. Vineyard tending and winemaking are done with a mix of ancient and modern methods. The grapes are harvested by machine, fermentation in plastic-lined concrete vats lasts for about 10 days, the wines spend 14 months in Nevers and Allier 58.5-gallon *barriques* before bottling.

The benefits of a complete replanting of the vineyard bore fruit in a string of excellent vintages in the 1980s, notably a superb 1983, a classic long-flavored 1986, and a sumptuous 1989. As the vines aged further in the 1990s, a refined, richly aromatic quality one associates with the finest wines of Margaux was increasingly evident. D'Angludet has always been one of the best buys in Bordeaux and very fairly priced. Indeed, Peter Sichel often sounded like a lone voice of sanity in the madly speculative world of late-1990s Bordeaux: he felt strongly that the skyrocketing prices reached by classed growth chateaux in the 1996 *en primeur* campaign could kill the goose that laid the golden egg before the end of the century, as it had done in 1991–1994 and even more dramatically in 1974. We will not see his like again.

The duckpond at Château d'Angludet.

MARQUES DE GRINON

Head office: c/Alfonso XI, no. 12, 28014 Madrid, Spain
Tel: (34-91) 531 06 09 Fax: (34-91) 531 06 78
*Visitors to Dominio de Valepusa, Pusa Valley, Toledo Province:
by appointment*

*C*arlos Falcó, Marques de Griñon, is one of the pioneers in the modernization of wine-growing and making in Spain. After graduating in agricultural science at Louvain University, Belgium, and subsequently at Davis in California, in 1974 he introduced the Cabernet Sauvignon and Merlot grape varieties into Spain. These were followed by the Chardonnay, Petit Verdot, and Syrah varieties. Falcó belongs to one of Spain's oldest families. Since 1292, his family and title have been linked to the Dominio de Valdepusa in Toledo province.

At Valdepusa, 35 miles from Toledo, Falcó farms a vineyard of 125 acres in production. Cabernet Sauvignon covers the greater part of this area. The Marques

FACT BOX

OWNER: Carlos Falcó, Marques de Griñon

WINEMAKER: Carlos Falcó

TOTAL ANNUAL PRODUCTION:
8,500 cases

SIZE OF VINEYARD: 125 acres

GRAPE VARIETIES: Cabernet Sauvignon, Merlot

PERCENTAGE OF NEW WOOD:
varies according to vintage

BEST RECENT VINTAGE: 1994

BEST DISHES TO MATCH WINES:
roast Castilian suckling pig

de Griñon Cabernet Reserva is, in fact, blended with 10 percent Merlot. Both varieties have an average age of 20 years. After fermentation in stainless-steel tanks, the wine is matured in French oak casks for 18–24 months. In a new association with the important Berberana group, Falcó has made a personal selection of Rioja made only from very old Tempranillo vines under a Marques de Griñon, Private Reserve label.

Carlos Falcó, Marques de Griñon, enjoying one of his fine wines.

Some of the large range of wines available from
Marques de Griñon.

CHATEAU DE LAMARQUE

33460 Lamarque, France
Tel: (33-5) 56 58 90 03 Fax: (33-5) 56 58 93 43
*Visitors: Monday–Friday 9:30AM–12 NOON
and 2:00PM–5:00PM*

*T*he ancient property of Lamarque was so named because it formed a border bastion to defend the Médoc against the invasion of the Vikings advancing up the Gironde. Around the primitive fortress, the château, still in existence today, was built in the fourteenth century with dungeons, defense towers, battlements, and crenellated walls. In 1841, the château was acquired by the Comte de Funel, a descendant of an old family from Quercy, and it is his great-great-grandson, Pierre-Gilles Gromond-Brunet d'Evry, who is now responsible for the wine production.

FACT BOX

OWNER: Pierre Gilles Gromond d'Evry

WINEMAKER: Jacques Boissenot

SIZE OF VINEYARD: 125 acres

TOTAL ANNUAL PRODUCTION:
25,000 cases

GRAPE VARIETIES: Cabernet Sauvignon, Merlot, Cabernet Franc, Petit Verdot

AVERAGE AGE OF VINES: 28 years

PERCENTAGE OF NEW WOOD:
65 percent

BEST RECENT VINTAGES: 1996, 1995

BEST DISHES TO MATCH WINES:
roasted meats, poultry, mushrooms, cheeses

LOCAL RESTAURANT: Le Lion d'Or, Areins

Pierre-Gilles Gromond moves between the milieu of Bordeaux and the high-tech world of modern France with great ease, for he is president of the powerful Gromond d'Evry group of engineering companies. They have financed his complete renovation of the vineyards and winery. Lamarque is now one of the very best *crus bourgeois* in the Médoc, a model operation producing excellent classic clarets that punch well above their weight.

> ## TASTING NOTES
>
> ### CHATEAU DE LAMARQUE 1995
>
> Drunk in 1995 from a magnum, a memorable wine. Deep ruby, with only the slightest trace of garnet-rimmed evolution; sumptuously rich on nose and palate, with all the fruit of a hot summer, but all within a superb classic structure; long minerally end flavor. Lovely.
>
> Rating ★★★★

The grapes are picked when fully mature, by variety and by separate vineyard parcels. For 25 years the vinification has been carried out under the supervision of Professor Emile Peynaud and his protégé Jacques Boissenot, an exceptional oenologist. Each grape variety is fermented separately and vatting usually lasts for 21 days, with extremely precise temperature control and constant submerging of the cap of fermenting grapes. The entire production is put into Allier oak barrels for 18–20 months. The percentage of new oak is usually two-thirds new and one-third one-year-old barrels. The 1985, drunk in magnums in 1995, was a spectacular wine, with all the flesh and charm of that vintage allied to a tremendous depth of flavor one associates more with a 1982 or 1961. The 1996 looks set to be another exceptional wine. Lamarque should be on every claret lover's shopping list, as it offers unbeatable quality and value for money.

The fourteenth century Château de Lamarque.

DOMAINE DE LA POUSSE D'OR

Rue de la Chapelle, 21190 Volnay, France
Tel: (33-3) 80 21 61 33 Fax: (33-3) 80 21 29 97
Visitors: by appointment

*O*utsiders usually bring an open mind to a new career, and Gérard Potel's arrival at this old *domaine* in 1964 was like a gust of fresh air. Having started life as a farmer in the Aisne, he had no preconceptions about winemaking and so rapidly became a courageous pacesetter and a force for better red Burgundy. He was, for example, one of the first growers to discard imperfect grapes at harvest time in order to ensure that his *domaine*-bottled wines were of a high standard each year. At the end of the twentieth century, his is a model estate and one of the surest sources of great

FACT BOX

OWNER: SCA Domaine de la Pousse d'Or

WINEMAKER: Gérard Potel

SIZE OF VINEYARD: 32.5 acres

TOTAL ANNUAL PRODUCTION: 6,000 cases

GRAPE VARIETY: Pinot Noir

AVERAGE AGE OF VINES: 25 years

PERCENTAGE OF NEW WOOD: 33–50 percent, depending on vintage

BEST RECENT VINTAGES: 1996, 1995, 1993, 1991

BEST DISHES TO MATCH WINES: *caneton aux cerises*; lightly hung game, especially woodcock

LOCAL RESTAURANT: Ma Cuisine, Beaune

Volnay. The *domaine* owns some of the finest sites in the commune and is the largest proprietor of Les Caillerets, which includes its monopole, the Clos des 60 Ouvrées. Gerard's home is a beautiful house, hewn out of a Volnay hillside, with deep, cool cellars and an enchanting flower-filled terrace overlooking the vineyards.

TASTING NOTES

VOLNAY CLOS DES 60 OUVREES 1991

Very fine translucent color with hints of vermilion; soaring Volnay aromas, delicate but persistent; concentrated but neither too extracted or overwooded flavors; silky finish of the highest class. *Grand vin.*
Rating ★★★★

The key to the exceptional quality of these wines is an intelligent respect for the character of each vintage, supported by the most modern techniques. For example, Gérard is experimenting with a *Durafroid* machine that evaporates the water on the grapes, obviating the need to chaptalize the wines in rainy years. Such attention to detail gives the best possible chance of achieving well-balanced, pure flavors, vintage after vintage. The *domaine* is now well known for the excellence of its wines in so-called off years … In recent excellent vintages, such as 1996 and 1993, they are outstanding, a benchmark of silken elegance and firm structure.

Like several progressive winemakers on the Côte, Gérard keeps a watchful eye on the New World. He has now gone one stage further in a joint venture in Western Australia, where Pinot Noir vines have been planted. Once the vineyard has matured, it will be fascinating to see if Gérard's light touch can tame the great red Burgundy grape grown in a very hot climate.

Gérard Potel's enchanting house on his estate in Volnay.

CHATEAU DE PEZ

33180 St. Estèphe, France
Tel: (33-5) 56 59 30 26
Visitors: by appointment only

*F*ounded in the fifteenth century, the Domaine of Pez is one of the two oldest estates in St. Estèphe. The Pontac family (*qv*), the creators of Haut-Brion, planted the vineyard in 1750. This has been one of the very best Médoc *crus bourgeois*, producing wines of classed-growth standard in a classic, full-bodied, and long-lived style. The superb 1970 outshone a 1967 Château Latour at a Ban de Vendange dinner in 1992.

Apart from an excellent Cabernet-dominated 1986, some recent vintages were lackluster. But in 1995, the château and vineyard were bought by Champagne Louis Roederer, so we may expect a return to top

FACT BOX

OWNER: Champagne Louis Roederer
WINEMAKER: Jean-Baptiste Lecaillon
SIZE OF VINEYARD: 60 acres
TOTAL ANNUAL PRODUCTION:
12,000 cases
GRAPE VARIETIES: Cabernet Sauvignon 45 percent; Merlot 8 percent; Cabernet Franc 3 percent; Petit Verdot 3 percent
AVERAGE AGE OF VINES: over 30 years
PERCENTAGE OF NEW WOOD:
40 percent
BEST RECENT VINTAGE: 1996
BEST DISHES TO MATCH WINES:
meat, game
LOCAL HOTEL/RESTAURANT:
Château Cordeillan Bages, Pauillac

TASTING NOTE

CHATEAU DE PEZ
1994

Ruby color with mauve
highlights; fine intense nose,
ripe red fruits, a hint of toast;
elegant yet full flavor,
with good concentration
and mellow tannins;
silky mouthfeel.

Rating ★★★

form in view of the considerable sums being spent in modernizing the winery.

The vineyard dominates a high plateau with well-exposed slopes. The soil is composed of Gunzian gravel overlying the limestone/clay bedrock of St. Estèphe; the significant presence of clay in particular gives the wine its staying power. In the winemaking, de Pez remains resolutely faithful to wood; fermentation on the skins in old open-top oak vats lasts for 21 days. The blend is composed in December, then the wine is stored in barrels (40 percent new wood) and racked every three months. After about a year, roughly halfway through its period of barrel maturation, the wine is fined with white of egg. It is never filtered. A classic de Pez shows deep color and a richness and denseness of flavor meriting prolonged aging. Great vintages are rarely at their peak before 12 to 15 years.

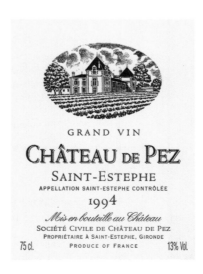

GRAND VIN

CHÂTEAU DE PEZ
SAINT-ESTEPHE
APPELLATION SAINT-ESTEPHE CONTRÔLÉE
1994
Mis en bouteille au Château
SOCIÉTÉ CIVILE DE CHÂTEAU DE PEZ
PROPRIÉTAIRE À SAINT-ESTEPHE, GIRONDE
75 cl.   PRODUCE OF FRANCE   13% Vol.

CHATEAU DES JACQUES, MOULIN A VENT

71570 Romaneche-Thorins, France
Tel: (33-3) 80 20 19 57 Fax: (33-3) 80 22 56 03
Visitors: by appointment only

*T*arnished by association with the mass of dull Beaujolais-Nouveau, the top wines (*crus*) from the northern Beaujolais hills are now seriously underrated and out of fashion. This is especially true of Moulin-à-Vent, where the brown soils rich in manganese can produce deeply colored, structured red wines akin to good Burgundy. All that is required is traditional winemaking and the patience to allow the wines to age properly. The Château des Jacques has always been the preeminent Moulin-à-Vent property, using completely traditional methods. So when the estate, long owned by the Thorin family,

FACT BOX

OWNERS: Maison Louis Jadot

WINEMAKER: Pierre de Boissieu

SIZE OF VINEYARD: 90 acres

TOTAL ANNUAL PRODUCTION: 30,000 cases

GRAPE VARIETY: Gamay Noir

AVERAGE AGE OF VINES: 35 years

PERCENTAGE OF NEW WOOD: 50 percent

BEST RECENT VINTAGES: 1996, 1995

BEST DISHES TO MATCH WINES: offal, especially kidneys; cow's milk cheeses

LOCAL HOTEL/RESTAURANT: Les Maritonnes, Romaneche-Thorins

changed hands in January 1997, it was lucky to be bought by the blue-chip Beaune house of Louis Jadot, a firm wealthy and enlightened enough to take a similarly long-term view.

Under the new ownership, the vineyards extend to 67.5 acres entitled to the Moulin-à-Vent *appellation* and 22.5 acres of white grapes that may be made into wine labeled Beaujolais or Macon *blanc*. The manager and winemaker, Pierre de Boissieu, is adapting slightly the way in which the red grapes are handled when they arrive at the vat-house: 80 percent of the grapes will be de-stalked (a method unique in Beaujolais to this property), but 20 percent will retain their stalks to ease the flow of fermentation. The traditional fermentation, involving regular pumping-over of the juice to moisten the grape skins and encourage the development of tannins, lasts for 14–21 days at temperatures of up to 89.6°F. A particularly interesting feature is that the red wines from particular vineyard sites within the estate are vinified in vats, aged in small oak *barriques*, and bottled separately; the range of finished wines thus encompasses six *cuvées*, each named after its originating site, in addition to a generic Château des Jacques bottling, which is a blend of wines from all the vineyards.

> ### TASTING NOTES
>
> #### CHATEAU DES JACQUES, ROCHEGRES, 1996
>
> From the highest point in the *appellation* (Chenas), a dark, rich, ruby wine, packed with ripe tannins and acidity, but with deep wells of fruit, in no way stalky. Very long-flavored. Outstanding. Put away and drink from 2000 to 2005.
>
> Rating ★★★★

A tasting at the estate in September 1997 of the excellent 1996 vintage vividly illustrated the varied character of the wines from different sites. The dark, ruby-red *Les Thorins* is medium-weight, smooth, fleshy, very Burgundian; *Le Champ de Coeur* is fine and long-flavored, needing time; *Grand Carquelin*, very aromatic (violets) and evolved, is the most typically Beaujolais; *La Roche* is a very pure Gamay fruit with notes of wild mushrooms and a discreet touch of vanilla; and grandest of all, *Rochegres* (*see* Tasting Notes) is a real keeper for long cellaring. These wines are excellent value for Burgundy lovers with Ferrari tastes on Ford budgets.

A. & P. DE VILLAINE

2 rue de la Fontaine, 71150 Bouzeron, France
Tel: (33-3) 85 91 20 50 Fax: (33-3) 85 87 04 10
*Visitors: by appointment only, weekdays 9:00AM–12 NOON
and 2:00PM–5:00PM*

*A*ubert de Villaine is best known as the part-owner and full-time director of the Domaine de la Romanée-Conti, Burgundy's most famous estate. One of the wine trade's great gentlemen, de Villaine is the most courteous and informative of growers, always ready to give full and honest answers to the endless questions fired at him by the world's wine press. It is typical of the man that he should live with his American wife Pauline in Bouzeron, a quiet village of Burgundy's hinterland, 10 minutes' drive away from the sleepy town of Chagny.

FACT BOX

OWNERS: A. & P. de Villaine

WINEMAKER: Aubert de Villaine

SIZE OF VINEYARD: 50 acres

TOTAL ANNUAL PRODUCTION:
12,000 cases

GRAPE VARIETY: Pinot Noir
(La Digoine)

AVERAGE AGE OF VINES: 20 years

PERCENTAGE OF NEW WOOD:
10–15 percent

BEST RECENT VINTAGES: 1996, 1995,
1993, 1990

BEST DISHES TO MATCH WINES:
roast pigeon, red meats

LOCAL RESTAURANTS:
Lameloise, Chagny; Hostêllerie du Val
d'Or, Mercurey

Bouzeron is known for its Aligoté. On the southeast-facing, limestone/clay slopes above the village, this workhouse white grape is transformed into a valuable source of slaty, dry, light-bodied, and elegant white wine for early drinking. De Villaine makes the best Aligoté in the village. Yet his red wine, the Bourgogne rouge "La Digoine," is even more remarkable.

This 100 percent Pinot Noir is made with the same perfectionist care as his *grands crus* of the DRC. The culture of the vines has been entirely organic for the last 10 years; compost is the only fertilizer used, herbicides are not. The grapes are picked by hand, fermentation takes place in open vats for 12 to 15 days, and the wines are then aged in wooden barrels, of which only 10 to 15 percent are new. De Villaine once told me he detected a taste of raspberries and truffles in La Digoine. Certainly he has caught all the aroma, fruit, and finesse of Burgundy Pinot Noir in a bottle costing less than $15–no mean achievement. One of Burgundy's great values.

> ## TASTING NOTES
>
> ### BOURGOGNE ROUGE LA DIGOINE 1995
>
> Elegant, bright ruby, classic young Pinot Noir color; wild raspberry aroma, very pretty; beautifully pure fruit with an end note of earth, mushrooms, and, yes, truffles. Considerable class for little outlay.
>
> Rating ★★★★

A. ET P. DE VILLAINE
Propriétaires à Bouzeron
Bourgogne
Aligoté de Bouzeron
Appellation Contrôlée
RECOLTE
1996
Mis en bouteilles au Domaine
12,5% vol.   e 75 cl.
Product of France

A. ET P. DE VILLAINE
Propriétaires à Bouzeron
Bourgogne
CÔTE CHALONNAISE
Les Clous
Appellation Bourgogne Contrôlée
RECOLTE
1995
Mis en bouteilles au Domaine
12,5% vol.   e 75 cl.
Product of France

DOMAINE DROUHIN, OREGON

Breyman Orchards Road, Dundee, Oregon 97115, USA
Tel: (1-503) 864 2700 Fax: (1-503) 864 3372
Visitors: by appointment only

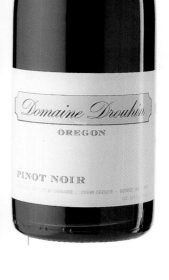

*S*ince the release of its first vintage in 1988, Domaine Drouhin has been acclaimed as the yardstick producer of Pinot Noir in Oregon. The consistent excellence of these wines owes everything to Véronique Drouhin, the winemaker, who combines a mastery of modern technology with an intimate knowledge of the classic French wine tradition.

Born in 1962 on the day of the Hospice de Beaune Sale, Véronique is the daughter of Robert Drouhin, the distinguished Burgundy shipper and vineyard owner (*see* Maison Joseph Drouhin page 76). After taking two degrees in oenology at the University of Dijon, Véronique trained at Château Fieuzal in the Pessac-

FACT BOX

OWNER: Robert Drouhin
WINEMAKER: Véronique Boss-Drouhin
SIZE OF VINEYARD: 180 acres
TOTAL ANNUAL PRODUCTION: 10,000 cases
GRAPE VARIETY: Pinot Noir (100 percent)
AVERAGE AGE OF VINES: 9 years
PERCENTAGE OF NEW WOOD: 20 percent
BEST RECENT VINTAGE: 1993
BEST DISHES TO MATCH WINES: chicken, lamb, beef; also excellent with salmon

Leognan (Graves) district of Bordeaux. She joined Maison Drouhin in 1987 and became closely involved in vinification and daily tastings of present and older vintages with her father. As part of her studies, Véronique had made a special analysis of the opportunities and challenges of winemaking in the Pacific Northwest, so when Robert Drouhin decided to launch his first and only winemaking venture outside Burgundy, Oregon was chosen as the ideal place to make Pinot Noir.

TASTING NOTES

DOMAINE DROUHIN OREGON PINOT NOIR 1994

Bright, elegant ruby with vermilion tints; very pure cherry fruit, a touch of vanilla; silky, well-defined flavor, good length. Immaculate.

Rating ★★★

The estate is located on a south-facing slope in the Red Hills of the Willamette Valley, 30 miles southwest of Portland. The same gentle perfectionist treatment of the grapes and the wine that the Drouhins employ for the greatest red Burgundies was applied to their new Pinot child from the start. The grapes are picked by hand in small 25-pound boxes; fermentation starts naturally with indigenous yeasts; the cap is traditionally punched down for full but sensitive color extraction; and, as the winery is built on a hill, maximum use of gravity is employed when racking the young wine to preserve its aromatic potential. The use of new wood is never higher than 20 percent so that the mouthwatering Pinot Noir fruit is not upstaged by the oak.

Véronique Drouhin, winemaker at Domaine Drouhin.

The stunning landscape from the vineyards at
Domaine Drouhin.

The Domaine produces two wines in most vintages. The flagship DD Oregon Pinot Noir, although structured and long-flavored, is intended to give immediate pleasure on release, with purity of fruit and a silky texture the main impressions. The DD Oregon Laurene Pinot Noir, named after Véronique's eldest daughter, is more complex, fuller, and set for a long life. Of the nine vintages made so far, the Drouhins rate the 1993 their best effort.

GEORGES DUBOEUF

B.P. 12, 71570 Romaneche-Thorins, France
Tel: (33-3) 85 35 34 20 Fax: (33-3) 85 35 34 20
Visitors: Le Hameau du Vin *wine museum and park,*
open daily during working hours

*F*rom small acorns great oak trees grow. Georges Duboeuf is the greatest merchant in Beaujolais, his firm now accounting for 15 percent of the region's wine sales worldwide, and all achieved in just over 30 years. As a young physical education student in Paris in the 1950s, Georges grew bored with traveling to the gym every day on the subway, so he returned to his family's small vineyard in Pouilly Fuisse, near Macon. From modest beginnings, he gradually developed a serious restaurant clientele for his wine, drawn from the pages of the *Michelin Guide.* At the start of the 1960s

FACT BOX

OWNERS: Les Vins Georges Duboeuf
WINEMAKERS: Georges and Franck Duboeuf
SIZE OF VINEYARD: 180 acres
TOTAL ANNUAL PRODUCTION: 1 million cases
GRAPE VARIETY: Gamay
EXCLUSIVE DISTRIBUTOR OF: Fleurie Domaine des Quatre Vents
AVERAGE AGE OF VINES: 30 years
PERCENTAGE OF NEW WOOD: 10 to 20 percent
BEST RECENT VINTAGES: 1996, 1995
BEST DISHES TO MATCH WINES: *charcuterie,* offal, and creamy cheeses
LOCAL RESTAURANT: Les Maritonnes, Romaneche-Thorins

he went into partnership with Paul Bocuse and Alexis Lichine in a venture that sought to promote growers' Beaujolais and Maconnais wines, but the growers could never agree on a common strategy and, in 1964, Georges established his own company, Les Vins Georges Duboeuf at Chanes.

Georges has always been a very gifted communicator, getting the clear message across to world markets that true Beaujolais can be the most delicious wine—fresh, floral, and free from any trace of bitterness. His success has been based on fair prices, superb contemporary presentation, and the best modern vinification techniques. Georges is a workaholic, up at

> ### TASTING NOTE
> #### FLEURIE DOMAINE DES QUATRE VENTS 1996
> Bright purple ruby, floral bouquet typical of Fleurie; silky mouthfeel, with great purity of Gamay fruit. Good acidity. Will improve until 1999.
> Rating ★★★

5:30 every morning, in his office by 6:00, ready to give advice to a grower or to try a new *cuvée*. In fact, he and his son Franck taste more than 7,000 wines a year from 300 Beaujolais growers. And whatever jealous competitors may say, each of the selected wines that carry the Duboeuf label is a very good example of its village and *appellation*. The man has entrenched himself in the culture of Beaujolais and is trusted completely by many growers, who have dealt with him without a contract from the beginning. Ever the realist, Georges has been quick to see that the boon of Beaujolais Nouveau, which brought prosperity to the region in the 1970s and 1980s, is now a potential curse, encouraging greedy growers to overproduce wine, thereby tarnishing the reputation of the famous *crus* from the northern hills of the region. In the 1990s, the firm has diversified its wine interests with the acquisition of a vineyard in the northern Rhône at Côte Rôtie and a second, larger one in the neighboring Ardèche, where a delicious Viognier *blanc* is made.

Georges Duboeuf, the "King of Beaujolais."

CLOS DU VAL

5330 Silverado Trail, P.O. Box 4350,
Napa, California 94558, USA
Tel: (1-707) 259-2231 Fax: (1-707) 252-6125
Visitors: by appointment

*F*ounded in 1972, this Stag's Leap winery quickly gained a reputation for the very high quality of its Cabernet Sauvignon wines. Early on, Clos du Val showed that balance is more important than power in a fine wine, and these Cabernets have always combined rich Napa fruit with an elegant French restraint. Hardly surprising, for the driving force here, the founding winemaker and chief executive, is Bernard Portet, a Frenchman brought up in Bordeaux, where his father was the technical director of Château Lafite-Rothschild.

The Clos du Val Cabernet Reserve is still one of the greatest red wines of California,

FACT BOX

OWNERS: Clos du Val Wine Co. Ltd.
WINEMAKER AND CHIEF EXECUTIVE: Bernard M. Portet
SIZE OF VINEYARD: 400 acres
TOTAL ANNUAL PRODUCTION: 80,000 cases
GRAPE VARIETY: Cabernet Sauvignon
AVERAGE AGE OF VINES: 15 years
PERCENTAGE OF NEW WOOD: upward of 50 percent, depending on vintage
BEST RECENT VINTAGES: 1996, 1994, 1992, 1991
BEST DISHES TO MATCH WINES: roast lamb or pork
LOCAL RESTAURANTS: Napa Valley Grill & Bistro, Don Giovanni

for it ages better than most due to the inherent excellence and structure of the finest Stag's Leap grapes and to the skillful art of blending a little Merlot with the Cabernet, thus preserving the wine's fruit into old age. If you ever see the superb 1987 Reserve at auction, don't hesitate to buy it once you have satisfied yourself that the wine is in good condition and has a traceable history of being well stored.

The run of excellent vintages 1990–1996 is a true embarrassment of riches; if one has to make a choice, the majestic tannins of the 1996 will allow this Cabernet Reserve to live a very long, distinguished life, and the 1991, benefiting from an exceptionally long growing season, is an exquisitely refined wine. I personally like the 1993 (*see* Tasting Notes), as this Cabernet could only have been made by a Frenchman in California.

Clos du Val also makes excellent Chardonnay and very good Zinfandel. The Pinot Noir is very respectable and well structured.

> ## TASTING NOTES
> ### CLOS DU VAL CABERNET SAUVIGNON RESERVE 1993
>
> Deep lustrous ruby but not overextracted; generous rich aromas of blackcurrants; equally generous blackcurrant fruit on palate but with a fine subtle restraint too; excellent acidity, keeping something in reserve. A stylish wine for drinking 1999/2000.
>
> Rating ★★★

Bernard M. Porter,
President and winemaker

FAIRVIEW

P.O. Box 583, Paarl 7824, South Africa
Tel: (27-21) 863 2450 Fax: (27-21) 863 2591
*Visitors: Monday–Friday 8:00AM–5:00PM;
Saturday 8:30AM–1:00PM*

*F*airview is one of the Cape's most beautiful estates, with commanding views of Table Mountain. The original grant of land was made in 1693 by Simon Van Der Stel. The farm passed through numerous hands until 1936, when it was purchased by Charles Back's grandfather, who came to South Africa from eastern Europe.

Winemaking had already been established here for some time. It is said that a local doctor used to prescribe teaspoons of wine from the farm for poorly children. Nowadays, the wines of Fairview are more than medicinal; across the range in both

FACT BOX

OWNERS: Back family
WINEMAKER: Charles Back
SIZE OF VINEYARD: 412.5 acres
TOTAL ANNUAL PRODUCTION:
100,000 cases
GRAPE VARIETIES: Shiraz, Pinot Noir, Pinotage (major red varieties)
AVERAGE AGE OF VINES: 15 years
PERCENTAGE OF NEW WOOD:
upward of 30 percent
BEST RECENT VINTAGE: 1993
BEST DISHES TO MATCH WINES:
barbecues of beef and lamb, strong cheeses
LOCAL HOTEL/RESTAURANT:
Mount Nelson Hotel, Cape Town

The magnificent Paarl Valley across from Fairview.

colors they offer vivid, delicious flavors at keen prices, thanks to the economies of scale. Current annual production is about 100,000 cases. All this is the work of Charles Back, a complex character who is at once a passionate winemaker and natural entrepreneur. He is also a highly successful cheese producer, offering excellent Italian- and French-style goat and sheep cheeses, some of which are Kosher.

The vineyard, on the lower slopes of Paarl Mountain, extends for 412.5 acres over soils of decomposed granite and sandstone. These soils are ideal for growing Shiraz (Syrah) grapes. The Fairview Shiraz is a delightful wine, full of mulberry fruitiness but with a structure to allow it to age well. A consistent performer, laden down with gold

TASTING NOTES

FAIRVIEW SHIRAZ 1993

Deep, rich carmine red; gorgeous forward aromas of mulberries and baked fruitcake; palate confirms the northern Rhonish mulberry flavors of Syrah but without the strong tannins and the pepper. A crowd pleaser.

Rating ★★★★

The great tower and cellar at Fairview.

medals, it has been successful in every vintage since 1988. The 1993 is outstanding. Fairview also makes excellent Pinotage (the crossbreed South African grape variety), with none of the whiff of nail polish that used to taint this wine in the Cape. Of the whites, the Semillon is a lovely full wine, great with sweetbreads.

Charles Back, Winemaker at Fairview

HAMILTON RUSSELL VINEYARDS

Hemel-en-Aarde Valley, P.O. Box 158, Hermanus,
Cape 7200, South Africa
Tel: (27-283) 23595 Fax: (27-283) 21797
Visitors: weekdays 9:00AM–5:00PM, Saturdays 9:00AM–1:00PM

*T*here are probably more loose words written about Pinot Noir than any other grape variety. According to traditionalists, only in the climate, rocks, and soil of Burgundy's Côte d'Or can this capricious grape really show its full potential in outstanding red wine. The "only here" claim made by many Burgundians is misleading and complacent, for the current reality is that a small band of winemakers around the world are increasing making very

FACT BOX

OWNER: Anthony Hamilton Russell

WINEMAKER: Kevin Grant

SIZE OF VINEYARD: 160 acres

TOTAL ANNUAL PRODUCTION:
25,000 cases (including Pinot Noir, Chardonnay, and Sauvignon Blanc)

GRAPE VARIETIES: Pinot Noir, Chardonnay

AVERAGE AGE OF VINES: 12 years (Barbaresco vineyards)

PERCENTAGE OF NEW WOOD: about 30 percent (depending on vintage)

BEST RECENT VINTAGES: 1997, 1996, 1991

BEST DISHES TO MATCH WINES: for Pinot Noir, venison and roast duck with berries

LOCAL RESTAURANT: Burgundy Restaurant, Hermanus

respectable Pinot Noir wines that give a good deal more pleasure than a lot of also-ran red Burgundies do.

The problem is that the generality of Pinot Noir outside Burgundy, particularly those wines from Napa and Sonoma, tend to have an overt fruitiness, a headiness, an extraction of color and flavor that may make them crowd-pleasers, but when judged against the delicacy and tranquil intensity of the greatest wines of a top grower in Chambolle-Musigny or Volnay, they are quite outclassed.

Will they always be? I wouldn't bank on it, judging by the ever-more subtle flavors wrought from Pinot Noir each year by the Hamilton Russell estate at the coolest and southernmost tip of the African continent. This is an enterprise that sets itself the highest possible standards. "We do not aim for bold, often short-lived, fruity immediacy, but for a concentrated complexity of character and potential for future development," says the owner, Anthony Hamilton Russell. "It is our goal that our wines should capture the romance of place and capture the drama of vintage." That may sound a little poetic but is another eloquent way of saying that the *terroir* of his Hemel-en-Aarde Valley vineyard is as important to Anthony as a parcel of Morey-St. Denis would be to a great Burgundy grower like Jacques Seysses.

I remember a visit to Hamilton Russell in October 1990 as if it were yesterday. The Hemel vineyard is one of the most beautiful I have ever seen, its

proximity to the southern Atlantic Ocean and the smell of herbs reminding me of Provence, but with an extra character that could only be African. Situated on northerly and northeasterly slopes, the vineyard has 16 types of low-vigor, stony soils. Just under two miles from Walker Bay, it enjoys a cool maritime climate similar to that of Santa Barbara on the central coast of California, another excellent place for growing Pinot Noir. All the grapes are hand-harvested into small crates, which then go to a sorting table before crushing. In the cellar, gentle treatment and traditional vinification are the rule, with a strong use of natural yeasts and the best *barriques* from top French coopers. The style of Hamilton Russell Pinot Noirs is more Burgundian than so-called "New World," with clear, translucent colors, fresh aromas becoming ethereal with age, tightly poised structure, and long, persistent flavors. But it is, of course, more than that, with an expression of its origins that is highly individual.

> ### TASTING NOTES
>
> ### HAMILTON RUSSELL PINOT NOIR 1996
>
> Very elegant, limpid vermilion-ruby; fine drawn aromas, more complex than any single identifiable fruit, with overlay of autumn leaves and Provençale herbs; close-knit on the palate, lovely Pinot expression, good acidity and length. Closed with a simple lever stopper, the wine still tasted good after a week (September 1997).
> Rating ★★★

Anthony candidly admits that the estate has had to cope with the problem of vine stock affected by leaf roll, but with the out-standing 1997 sourced by virus-free fruit coming on stream in 1998, Hamilton Russell is set to join the select company of the finest producers of Pinot Noir in the world. The estate also produces exceptional Chardonnay and very good Sauvignon Blanc.

DOMAINE MICHEL JUILLOT

B.P. 10 Grande Rue, 71640 Mercurey, France
Tel: (33-3) 85 45 27 27 Fax: (33-3) 85 45 25 52
*Visitors: daily except Sunday, 8:30AM–12:15PM,
2:00PM–6:00PM*

This is probably the best *domaine* in Mercurey and certainly the most dynamic. The eponymous Michel Juillot has doubled its size to 75 acres in less than 20 years without any compromise on quality. Since 1994, his able son Laurent has been the winemaker.

The *domaine* offers an interesting range of *premier cru* Mercureys from the *climats* of Clos des Barraults, Clos l'Evêque, Les Champs Martins and, a monopole of the *domaine*, Clos Tonnerre. Each has a real individuality of flavor, all share a very positive color and show a balance of

FACT BOX

OWNER: Michel Juillot
WINEMAKER: Laurent Juillot
SIZE OF VINEYARD: 75 acres
TOTAL ANNUAL PRODUCTION: 12,500 cases
GRAPE VARIETY: Pinot Noir
AVERAGE AGE OF VINES: 35 years
PERCENTAGE OF NEW WOOD: 15–20 percent
BEST RECENT VINTAGES: 1995, 1993, 1990
BEST DISHES TO MATCH WINES: *noisette* of roedeer, braised sweetbreads in vegetable *brunoise*
LOCAL HOTEL/RESTAURANT: Hôtellerie du Val d'Or, Mercurey

fruit, oak, and a distinctive minerality akin to a good Nuits St. Georges, but at a much more reasonable price. And, as if to show he can do better than his colleagues on the Côte d'Or, Michel now makes a powerful Corton Perrières from vines *en fermage*.

The winemaking at a modern *cuverie* in Mercurey is immaculate. The bunches of grapes are brought in whole and destalked. After first being cold-soaked for five days in order to obtain a good color, the grapes ferment in open-top, 17-fluid-ounce wooden vats for seven days at relatively high temperatures. After a further period of skin contact, the wine goes into barrel immediately so that the effect of the oak will be optimized during the malolactic fermentation. The amount of new oak used is sparing and judicious, ranging from 10 to 20 percent depending on the character of the vintage.

For the new millenium, Michel is releasing a special wine made from 70-year-old vines in the 1988 vintage. Called Mercurey 2000, it is available only in magnums.

> ## TASTING NOTES
>
> ### MERCUREY CLOS TONNERRE 1995
>
> A big wine to keep until 1999, preserving deep flavors alongside the stylish elegance and finesse typical of Juillot's wines; the ruby color is not too forced; on nose and palate a fine mix of little red fruits and notes of game, silky tannins, long finish. Immaculate.
> Rating ★★★

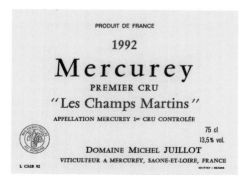

PRODUIT DE FRANCE

1992

Mercurey

PREMIER CRU

"Les Champs Martins"

APPELLATION MERCUREY 1er CRU CONTROLÉE

75 cl
13,5% vol.

DOMAINE MICHEL JUILLOT

VITICULTEUR A MERCUREY, SAONE-ET-LOIRE, FRANCE

L CMB 92

LEEUWIN ESTATE

Stevens Road, Margaret River, Western Australia 6285
Tel: (61-9) 430 4099 Fax: (61-9) 430 5687
Visitors: daily 10:00AM–4:30PM

*L*eeuwin Estate is one of the five founding wineries in the Margaret River region of Western Australia. The land where Leeuwin's vineyard now stands was identified in 1972 by American vintner Robert Mondavi as being ideal for the production of fine wine. It is not hard to see why. The summers are gently warm (at least by Australia's infernal standards), the land is bordered on three sides by the southern ocean, the gravel soils are similar to those of Bordeaux.

With Mondavi holding their hand, the Horgan family set about transforming their

FACT BOX

OWNERS: Denis and Tricia Horgan

WINEMAKER: Robert Cartwright

SIZE OF VINEYARD: 290 acres

TOTAL ANNUAL PRODUCTION:
500 tons

GRAPE VARIETIES: Cabernet Sauvignon 25 percent; Chardonnay 25 percent; Pinot Noir 10 percent; Sauvignon Blanc 12 percent; Riesling 28 percent

AVERAGE AGE OF VINES: 75 percent planted in 1974 and 1975; balance in 1994 and 1995

PERCENTAGE OF NEW WOOD:
100 percent

BEST RECENT VINTAGES: 1995, 1992, 1991, 1982

BEST DISHES TO MATCH WINES:
beef, lamb; game (Cabernet Sauvignon)

OWN RESTAURANT: Yes

cattle farm into a vineyard. A nursery was planted in 1974. The first trial vintage was in 1978. Twenty years on, Leeuwin ranks among the finest wineries in Australia and one of the top 20 in the New World. The estate's collection of modern Australian art that adorns the walls of the winery, its prestigious annual music concerts performed in the natural bushland amphitheater, and its award-winning restaurant all add a gloss to a very well-deserved reputation for producing outstanding Chardonnay.

The winery on the Leeuwin estate.

Critics tend to under-value the "Art Series" Cabernet Sauvignon, a very good wine by any standard. The fruit is harvested by machine and put into closed fermenters, where it is pumped over twice a day for color and tannin extraction. The fermentation and maceration period lasts for three weeks. The wine then matures for about 30 months in French oak and is rested for a further 14 months before release. With a great 1991, this rich yet classy wine came of age and was followed by an impressive 1992 and 1993.

DOMAINE JEAN MARÉCHAL

Grande Rue, 71640 Mercurey, France
Tel: (33-3) 85 45 11 29 Fax: (33-3) 85 45 18 52
*Visitors: Monday–Saturday 8:00AM–12 NOON
and 1:30–7:00PM, Sunday by appointment*

*T*he red wine of Mercurey regularly offers the canny buyer the best ratio of quality to price in the whole of Burgundy, this low-key *domaine* being one of its surest sources. The family have been winegrowers in the village since the late sixteenth century, so it is not surprising that the current generations, Jean Marechal and his son-in-law Jean-Marc Bovagne, make long-lived wines that require patient cellaring.

Here are all the ingredients for a classic bottle, fairly priced: 25 acres of mature vines situated on the best Mercurey slopes, sensible yields, handpicked grapes, traditional

FACT BOX

OWNER: Jean Marechal
WINEMAKERS: Jean Marechal and Jean-Marc Bovagne
SIZE OF VINEYARD: 25 acres
TOTAL ANNUAL PRODUCTION: 4,000 cases
GRAPE VARIETY: Pinot Noir
AVERAGE AGE OF VINES: 35 years
PERCENTAGE OF NEW WOOD: 10 percent
BEST RECENT VINTAGES: 1996, 1995, 1993
BEST DISHES TO MATCH WINES: grilled meats, poultry, and cheeses
LOCAL HOTEL/RESTAURANT: Hotellêrie du Val d'Or, Mercurey

treading-down (*pigeage*) of the cap of grapes, long, slow fermentations, a very sparing use of new wood. The top-of-the-range "Cuvée Prestige" is sourced from the *premier cru* grapes of Clos L'Evêque, Les Naugues, and Champs Martin. The 1993, from an exceptional year, is a real keeper with an intense aroma of cherries, the fine tannins contributing to the

> ### TASTING NOTES
> #### MERCUREY CUVEE PRESTIGE 1995
> Sustained deep-ruby color, very intense aromas of cherries with a note of raspberries; the tannins, at once fine yet powerful, promise a long life well into the twenty-first century.
> Rating ★★★★

wine's general harmony. The 1994 is more forward, vigorous yet fresh and delicate; the 1995 (*see* Tasting Notes) is a big wine for keeping until 2003–2005. The Marechals also make a fine-grained Mercurey *blanc* and good Bourgogne *rouge* for early drinking. The wines are sold mainly to private customers in France but are also exported to Germany and Great Britain.

The cellars at Mercurey.

Domaine Jean Marechal, Mercurey, France

CHATEAU MONBRISON

33460 Arsac, Margaux, France
Tel: (33-5) 56 58 80 94 Fax: (33-5) 56 58 85 33
Visitors: by appointment only

*T*his charming and romantic farmhouse, what the French call a *gentilhommière*, lies in secluded country behind Margaux within the commune of Arsac. The property and vineyard was bought in 1921 by the American poet and journalist Robert Davis, who lived here with his wife Kathleen (née Johnston) until 1939, when the vineyard was uprooted and the family went to live in Morocco for the duration of World War II. It was Davis's youngest daughter, Elizabeth, who resuscitated the estate and replanted the neglected vineyard in 1963.

FACT BOX

OWNER: Elizabeth Davis

WINEMAKER: Laurent Vonderheyden

SIZE OF VINEYARD: 32.5 acres

TOTAL ANNUAL PRODUCTION:
5,800 cases

GRAPE VARIETIES: Cabernet Sauvignon
50 percent; Merlot 30 percent;
Cabernet Franc 15 percent; Petit Verdot
5 percent

AVERAGE AGE OF VINES: 30 years

PERCENTAGE OF NEW WOOD:
up to 60 percent

BEST RECENT VINTAGES: 1996,
1995, 1990, 1989, 1988, 1986,
1985, 1983

BEST DISHES TO MATCH WINES:
red meat and game

LOCAL RESTAURANT:
Le Lion d'Or, Arcins

A farsighted move, for the vines are enviably sited on the same deep-gravel plateau, called Le Grand Poujeau, as Château d'Angludet (*qv*). The two wines share the same sturdy character and a burgeoning finesse and richness as the vines become really mature.

Monbrison is now a model operation, making one of the very best *crus bourgeois* in Bordeaux. Yields are admirably low, and the winemaking of

Elizabeth's son, Laurent Vonderheyden, is exemplary. Wine critics breathed a sigh of relief when Laurent proved himself a worthy successor in the *cuverie* to his brother, Jean-Luc, who died tragically young of leukaemia in 1992.

Vinification is very traditional, though conducted in enamel and stainless-steel tanks for optimal control. Fermentation temperatures are allowed to go as high as 89.6°F. The infant wine is pumped over twice a day with plenty of aeration, and can remain on the grape skins for 20–30 days before going in wooden barrels (up to 60 percent of which are new) for about two years. The finished wine

An aerial view of Château Monbrison, Margaux.

is firm and tannic, but with a latent silkiness and fine aroma that comes after seven to 10 years in bottle. Monbrison is Margaux at its most satisfying and refined, and consistently a much better wine than several classed growths within the *appellation*.

Chateau Montus

32400 Maumussin-Laguian, France
Tel: (33-5) 62 69 74 67 Fax: (33-5) 62 69 70 46
Visitors: Monday–Saturday 9:00AM–12 NOON and 2:00–6:30PM

The ebullient Alain Brumont is the Georges Duboeuf of southwest France, a man who has brought the forgotten red wine of Madiran to a wider world. Thirty years ago, Madiran was a bit of a bruiser, made essentially from the tough and tannic Tannat grape. Brumont's achievement has been to make it more supple and fine, through imaginative winemaking and the intelligent use of new wood. The regular bottling of his flagship Château Montus is a splendidly satisfying alternative to overpriced claret from up the road in the Gironde.

A former strategic defense of Castelnau-Rivière Basse, Château Montus was the

FACT BOX

OWNER: S.A. Domaines et Châteaux d'Alain Brumont

WINEMAKER: Alain Brumont

SIZE OF VINEYARD: 85 acres

TOTAL ANNUAL PRODUCTION: 16,000 cases

GRAPE VARIETIES: Tannat 80 percent; Cabernet Franc 10 percent; Cabernet Sauvignon 10 percent

AVERAGE AGE OF VINES: 15 years

PERCENTAGE OF NEW WOOD: 50 percent

BEST RECENT VINTAGES: 1995, 1990

BEST DISHES TO MATCH WINES: game dishes

LOCAL HOTEL/RESTAURANT: Hotel de France, Auch

TASTING NOTES

CHATEAU MONTUS
1994

Dark ruby color, vigorous and strong; powerful, sturdy, mouthfilling, but essentially well balanced, the tannins ripe, the flavors well rounded by just the right amount of new oak.
Drink end 1998 to 2001.
Rating ★★★

birthplace of the martyr Sainte-Liberate. The vineyard, reconstituted by Brumont in 1981, extends to 85 acres, predominantly Tannat with Cabernet Sauvignon and Fer Servadou. The soil on steep terraced slopes is composed of large pebbles atop a subsoil rich in iron and manganese–ideal for making strongly colored, powerful red wine. Everything is done, however, to bring finesse to Madiran's sturdy, at times roughly tannic, character: grapes are completely destemmed and long vatting times of 21 days at high temperatures of 86–95°F are employed; the wine spends 8 to 16 months in relatively new oak. Château Montus is a red wine for all seasons in the best sense of the word; you can either drink it with pleasure when young or keep it for up to 10 years, and it is also the most adaptable partner for dishes as disparate as *blanquette de vea*u and the finest game. There is also a majestic prestige bottling of Montus (superb 1990) made from 100 percent Tannat, though the regular *cuvée* remains better value for money.

PENLEY ESTATE

16 Ruthven Avenue, Adelaide, South Australia 5000
Tel: (61-8) 8231 2400 Fax: (61-2) 8231 0589
Visitors: by appointment

*T*he sixth generation of a distinguished family of South Australian winemakers, Kym Tolley worked for Penfolds before establishing the Penley Estate, Coonawarra, in 1988. A specialist in red wines, Tolley chose Coonawarra as the site of his vineyard because its combination of cool climate and rich red soils consistently produces Australia's most sumptuous yet finely balanced Cabernet Sauvignons. In just 10 vintages, the Penley Cabernets have come to the top of the class, with fruit, wood, and vinous complexity in textbook harmony.

FACT BOX

OWNER: Kim Tolley
WINEMAKER: Kim Tolley
SIZE OF VINEYARD: 205 acres
TOTAL ANNUAL PRODUCTION:
18,000 cases
GRAPE VARIETIES: Cabernet Sauvignon
56 percent; Shiraz 22 percent; Merlot
10 percent; Cabernet Franc 3 percent;
Pinot Noir 4 percent; Chardonnay
5 percent
AVERAGE AGE OF VINES: 8 years
PERCENTAGE OF NEW WOOD:
80 percent (Reserve Cabernet)
BEST RECENT VINTAGE: 1991
BEST DISHES TO MATCH WINES:
roast beef, lamb, grills, and game
LOCAL RESTAURANTS: Cobb & Co.,
The Hermitage; both in Coonawarra

TASTING NOTES

PENLEY ESTATE COONAWARRA RESERVE CABERNET SAUVIGNON 1992

Dense, rich ruby/purple color, no sign of age; lovely Coonawarra aromas, sweet plums and cream; palate has a serious structure and definition of long, elegant flavors. A fascinating wine, both a crowd pleaser and one for the connoisseur. Last tasted December 1997.

Rating ★★★★

COONAWARRA
PENLEY  ESTATE
AUSTRALIA

Penley grows all its Coonawarra grapes; none are bought in for the Reserve Cabernet Sauvignon label. The grapes are harvested by machine. Fermentation lasts for 7–10 days in stainless-steel tanks at cool temperatures of 64.4–68°F, the cap of fermenting grapes held down with wooden headboards for good extraction of color and fruit. The Reserve Cabernet is aged in both American and French oak. Because of its soft, rich flavor, this wine can be drunk relatively young but develops a mineral-like complexity after five to eight years in bottle.

Kym Tolley, founder of Penley Estate.

The Coonawarra vineyard at Penley Estate.

Penley also produces a fine brambly Shiraz, an easy drinking Cabernet/Shiraz, an impressive tightly-knit Chardonnay, and a *méthode champenoise* sparkling wine.

CHATEAU PICHON-
LONGUEVILLE (BARON)

33250 Pauillac, France
Tel: (33-5) 56 73 24 20 Fax: (33-5) 56 73 17 28
Visitors: by appointment

*S*ince its acquisition in 1987 by the powerful AXA insurance group, this historic Pauillac-classed growth has returned to top form after a long period in the doldrums. The château, which used to have no electricity or hot water, is now restored and provides sumptuous reception rooms and accommodation for the wine trade. The grand façade flanked by twin witch-hat towers always reminded me of the castle in Disney's *Snow White and the Seven Dwarfs*.

FACT BOX

OWNERS: AXA Millesimes

WINEMAKERS: Jean-Michel Cazes and Daniel Llose

SIZE OF VINEYARD: 125 acres

SECOND WINE: Les Tourelles de Longueville

TOTAL ANNUAL PRODUCTION: 24,000 cases

GRAPE VARIETIES: Cabernet Sauvignon 75 percent; Merlot 24 percent; Petit Verdot 1 percent

AVERAGE AGE OF VINES: 25 years

PERCENTAGE OF NEW WOOD: up to 70 percent

BEST RECENT VINTAGES: 1996, 1990

BEST DISHES TO MATCH WINES: *filet de boeuf en croûte*, roast grouse

LOCAL HOTEL/RESTAURANT: Château Cordeillan-Bages, Pauillac

The same cannot be said of the new winery. Ready for the 1992 vintage, this futuristic complex dominates the D2 *route des Châteaux*, more resembling the rocket control center at Cape Canaveral than the vat-house of a classed growth. But like it or loathe it, the complex is brilliantly designed for the making of

The newly restored Château at Pichon-Longueville.

great claret. All movement of wine is achieved by natural gravity. The pressed grape juice and skins drop down directly into stainless steel tanks for the fermentation; the infant wine then descends into *barriques* for the period of wood aging. There is no need to use pumps that might have a harmful oxidative effect on the wines. Other reforms introduced by the current directors, Jean-Michel Cazes and Daniel Llose of Château Lynch-Bages (*qv*), include late harvesting of the grapes by hand to achieve maximum ripeness, and increasing the proportion of new wood to 70 percent in great vintages.

Under the Cazes-Llose regime, Pichon Baron (as it is called, to distinguish it from Pichon Comtesse) is again making wines which fully live up to its high rank in the 1855 classification; these are classic Pauillacs—power and breed in complete balance. First-rate vintages were made in 1988, 1989, and especially 1990 when only the mighty Château Latour (*qv*) was ahead of Pichon by a short head. Les Tourelles de Longueville, Pichon's second wine, is usually an excellent buy, offering a faster maturing version of the *grand vin* at a relatively reasonable price.

> ## TASTING NOTES
>
> ### CHATEAU PICHON-LONGUEVILLE 1990
>
> Superb deep ruby color; a glorious nose of blackcurrant, minerals and "cigar-box" (classic Pauillac); great concentration of fruit and burgeoning vinous flavors beautifully balanced with oak; an exceptionally long finish. A great wine which will improve until 2010.
> Rating ★★★★★

CHATEAU POUJEAUX

33480 Moulis en Médoc, France
Tel: (33-5) 56 58 02 96 Fax: (33-5) 56 58 01 25
*Visitors: Monday–Saturday 9:00AM–12:00 NOON
and 2:00PM–5:00PM*

*I*f one were asked to name a claret that always punches above its weight, this would be it. Although not a classed growth, Poujeaux is a great wine and one of the Médoc's finest values. The story goes that when the late Georges Pompidou entertained his boss, Baron Elie de Rothschild (owner of Lafite), at the family bank in Paris, he served two unlabeled 1953 clarets, each decanted. Baron Elie thought he recognized one wine as Lafite and thanked his host for the kind thought. "You are actually drinking the Poujeaux," replied Pompidou.

FACT BOX

OWNERS: The Theil family

WINEMAKER: François Theil

SIZE OF VINEYARD: 130 acres

TOTAL ANNUAL PRODUCTION: 25,000 cases

GRAPE VARIETIES: Cabernet Sauvignon 50 percent; Merlot 40 percent; Cabernet Franc 5 percent; Petit Verdot 5 percent

AVERAGE AGE OF VINES: 30 years

PERCENTAGE OF NEW WOOD: 50 percent

BEST RECENT VINTAGES: 1996, 1995, 1990, 1988, 1986, 1985

BEST DISHES TO MATCH WINES: venison, partridge, roast duck, and goose

LOCAL RESTAURANT: Le Lion d'Or, Arcins

Located in the heart of Medoc, between Margaux and St. Julien, the Moulis *appellation* benefits from an exceptional natural environment. Château Poujeaux in particular has an uninterrupted vineyard of 130 acres planted on the finest out-crops of Gunz gravel, the ideal soil for the great wine estates of the region. Add to this the human factor of the Theil brothers, who are among the

most passionate and committed *vignerons* and winemakers in Bordeaux, and you have the recipe for something very special.

The Theils believe in picking the grapes as late as possible for optimal ripeness. The vat room houses wooden vats, epoxy resin-lined concrete vats and stainless-steel tanks, all thermoregulated. The length of fermentation and maceration is an exceptional six weeks on average. The wines of Château Poujeaux always have a deep, strong color, subtle aromas, and flavors marked by soft, mellow tannins that are never aggressive. The wines taste good

The barrel room at Château Poujeaux.

Poujeaux wines usually have a deep, strong color,
and subtle aromas.

when quite young, but really need a good 10 years to show their
splendor. The 1985 is a marvelously sensuous bottle, the 1990 a
classic; both the 1995 and 1996 are among the greatest wines of
each vintage.

TASTING NOTES

CHATEAU POUJEAUX 1994

A first-rate result in this
relatively good vintage; deep
color, a bouquet at once
powerful and unctuous;
ripe black fruits explode in
the mouth but are balanced
by fine tannins and a
brilliant use of oak.
Masterly winemaking.
Rating ★★★★

LA RIOJA ALTA

Apartado no. 20, 26200 Haro, Spain
Tel: (34-41) 31 04 07 Fax: (34-41) 31 26 54
Visitors: by appointment

ounded in 1890, this family firm owns 750 acres of vineyard in prime sites of the Rioja Alta. The average yield is an impressively restricted 1,003 gallons to the acre. Grapes are also purchased long-term from traditional growers. The company's only concessions to technology are the gleaming stainless steel tanks for fermentation. By contrast, maturation, in both barrel and bottle, follows traditional Riojan methods–long aging in American oak casks with hand racking every six months followed by prolonged bottle aging. The permanent reserves of

FACT BOX

OWNERS: La Rioja Alta S.A.

WINEMAKER: not applicable

SIZE OF VINEYARD: 750 acres

TOTAL ANNUAL PRODUCTION: 66,000 cases

GRAPE VARIETIES: Tempranillo, Garnacha, Mazuelo, Graciano

AVERAGE AGE OF VINES: information not available

PERCENTAGE OF NEW WOOD: 10 percent (American oak)

BEST RECENT VINTAGES: 1994, 1989, 1987, 1983, 1978

BEST DISHES TO MATCH WINES: venison, roast suckling pig

LOCAL RESTAURANT: Beethoven, Haro

wine at 6.4 million bottles is equivalent to eight years' annual sales, and represents one of the greatest ratios of stock/sales of any wine producer in the world. Quality comes first here, but it comes at a price.

Rioja Alta's top wines–the Gran Reservas 904 and 890–are wonderful creamy ethereal wines, but as the ever realistic Robert Parker puts it, "the demand for them by the best Spanish restaurants ensures that only tiny quantities leave the country." As is usually the case with a great Rioja *bodegas*, the best values here are the straight reservas, especially the widely available Vina Ardanza. The very successful 1989 Ardanza (*see* Tasting Notes) is a full vigorous wine with a very traditional, flattering note of sweet vanilla that comes from its 42 months' spell in American oak. It will live and improve well into the first years of the twenty-first century–not bad for a wine costing less than $15 a bottle.

SAINTSBURY

1500 Los Carneros Avenue, Napa, California, USA
Tel: (1-707) 252 0592 Fax: (1-707) 252 0595
Visitors: by appointment only, 10:00AM–4:00PM

"*B*eaune in the USA." This zany slogan printed on the turquoise sweatshirts of the Saintsbury winery is no empty phrase, for the supple, fragrant Pinot Noirs made here give as much pleasure as many a good red Burgundy. It was a very different story in 1977, when David Graves and Richard Ward met at Davis, the wine school of the University of California. At that time, California Pinot Noir was a bad joke: big, brutal, and tannic. So Dave and Dick, over a bottle of Morey St. Denis, dreamed of starting their own winery dedicated to disproving

FACT BOX

OWNERS: David Graves and Richard Ward

WINEMAKER: Byron Kosuge

SIZE OF VINEYARD: 50 acres

TOTAL ANNUAL PRODUCTION: 48,000 cases

GRAPE VARIETIES: Pinot Noir, Chardonnay

AVERAGE AGE OF VINES: 5–29 years

PERCENTAGE OF NEW WOOD: 25 percent (Garnet); 40 percent (Carneros); 55 percent (Reserve)

BEST RECENT VINTAGES: 1995, 1991

BEST DISHES TO MATCH WINES: grilled lamb, meaty fish (monkfish, tuna, salmon)

LOCAL RESTAURANTS: Celadon (Napa), French Laundry & Domaine Chandon (Yountville)

the notion that Pinot Noir from Napa was little better than jug wine.

They knew the choosy Burgundy grape didn't like heat, so after much searching they settled on Carneros, an old livestock grazing district straddling Napa and Sonoma, where the climate is dominated by the flow of cool marine air from the nearby Pacific Ocean and San Pablo Bay. The partners borrowed from family and friends and, in 1981, started making Pinot Noir and Chardonnay, first in an old rented winery in St. Helena and later at Los Carneros Avenue in a modern, wooden structure shaped like a barn. The venture was playfully named after the irascible British academic George Saintsbury, whose pontifications on the grape were holy writ during the 1920s. "We kind of liked the old codger," say the partners, tongue-in-cheek maybe, but with the shrewd calculation that the name is preeminently associated with good living. At the end of the twentieth century, Saintsbury is one of the most consistently stylish, dependable, and fairly priced sources of Pinot Noir in the world.

Byron Kosuge, Winemaker at Saintsbury.

Approximately 40 percent of its Pinot Noir needs come from Saintsbury's own vineyards; the remainder is grown by local farmers under supervision. The grapes are harvested by hand and completely destemmed. Vinification takes place in closed-top stainless-steel fermenters, small enough for ease of handling. Warm fermentation of Pinot Noir is considered essential, reaching temperatures of at least 120°F, making for a good extraction of color and tannin, and proper flavor development. Some new-oak character is a very important part of the Saintsbury house style but is never allowed to overwhelm the wines.

Three styles of Pinot Noir are produced: Garnet, a fresh, translucent wine full of primary orchard fruit flavors (marvelous with monkfish); Carneros Pinot Noir, a more classic rendition; and the Reserve Pinot Noir, the richest and fullest, a world-class wine, especially in both the classy, subtle 1991 and the ripe, intense 1995 vintages.

TASTING NOTES

SAINTSBURY RESERVE PINOT NOIR 1995

One of the most intense wines Saintsbury has made, but all beautifully balanced and complete. Deep but bright ruby, succulent rich and vinous nose, rich, chewy, with ripe tannins, mouthcoating but harmonious. Tasted against a Beaune *premier cru* 1995 from a top estate, this was the better wine. Last tasted September 1997.

Rating ★★★★

David Graves (left) and Dick Ward, founders of Saintsbury.

SHAFER VINEYARDS

6154 Silverado Trail, Napa, California 94558, USA
Tel: (1-707) 944 2877 Fax: (1-707) 944 9454
Visitors: by appointment Monday–Friday

*I*t is difficult for me to be objective here, for this is my favorite winery in California, founded and run by one of the most civilized men in the business. John Shafer, a children's book publisher from Chicago, bought the property in 1972. In a typically farsighted decision, he chose this hillside Stag's Leap vineyard, cooled by the afternoon breezes from San Francisco Bay, because he reckoned he would make finer wine here than in the more fashionable, flat-as-a-pancake Oakville Bench district of central Napa Valley. Thirty-five years

FACT BOX

OWNERS: John and Doug Shafer
WINEMAKER: Elias Fernandez
SIZE OF VINEYARD: 138 acres
TOTAL ANNUAL PRODUCTION: 30,000 cases
GRAPE VARIETIES: Cabernet Sauvignon, Merlot, Sangiovese, Chardonnay
AVERAGE AGE OF VINES: 12 years
PERCENTAGE OF NEW WOOD: 35 percent (for Merlot and Sangiovese), 60 percent (for Hillside Select)
BEST RECENT VINTAGES: 1994, 1990
BEST DISHES TO MATCH WINES: grilled salmon, duck's breast (Merlot), risotto, pasta (Firebreak); aged full-flavored cheese, roast beef (Hillside Select)
LOCAL RESTAURANT: Domaine Chandon, Yountville

John and Doug Shafer admiring the hills and vineyards
of Shafer in the Stags Leap district of Napa Valley.

on, he and his son Doug enjoy a thoroughly well-earned reputation
for making one of the finest ranges of wine in Napa. This is the
land of winemakers who believe that anything Bordeaux can do,
they can do better. In a class of rowdies, the Shafers are the quiet
men, confident in the excellence of their product but also relaxed
enough to write some of the funniest and least pretentious
wine newsletters around.

The Shafer estate now includes
53 acres around the winery and
Stag's Leap district, supplemented
by 68 acres in cool Carneros. This
latter acquisition is a major source
for the estate's increasingly impressive Chardonnays, finely oaked
wines of elegance and depth of flavor.
The real Shafer glories, though, are
the red wines. The Merlot is always
a sleek, bright wine, a wonderful

partner to duck. The Firebreak, made on the home vineyard, is an innovative Sangiovese-based blend with a touch of Cabernet Sauvignon, the family's answer to the Super Tuscans. The Hillside Select Cabernet Sauvignon is the pride of the cellar, a world-class red of concentration and savor that, in great vintages like 1994 and 1990, can hold its own in any company.

TASTING NOTES

CABERNET SAUVIGNON HILLSIDE SELECT 1994

Probably the best Hillside Select ever produced; dense purple/ruby color, magnificent scents of black fruits with mineral overtones; complete expression of ripe Cabernet Sauvignon, mouthfilling, fleshy, but beautifully balanced and pure flavored. Absolutely faultless.

Rating ★★★★★

CHATEAU TROPLONG MONDOT

33330 St. Emilion, France
Tel: (33-5) 57 55 32 05 Fax: (33-5) 57 55 32 07
Visitors: by appointment

*T*o the northeast of St.-Emilion, this fine old property is located on the bluff of Mondot, which rises to a height of over 300 feet and commands fine views of the surrounding countryside. The Troplong part of the name commemorates Raymond Troplong, the celebrated French senator, jurist, and patron of the arts who owned the château from 1852 to 1869 and made first-class wine here. Such excellence was not seen again until Christine Valette, with the help of the oenologist

FACT BOX

OWNER: G. F. Valette

WINEMAKER: Christine Valette

SIZE OF VINEYARD: 75 acres

SECOND WINE: Mondot

TOTAL ANNUAL PRODUCTION: 8,500 cases (*grand vin*)

GRAPE VARIETIES: Merlot 80 percent; Cabernet Franc 10 percent; Cabernet Sauvignon 10 percent

AVERAGE AGE OF VINES: 45 years

PERCENTAGE OF NEW WOOD: 70 percent

BEST RECENT VINTAGES: 1996, 1995, 1994, 1990

BEST DISH TO MATCH WINES: *canard rôti au fumet d'olives*

LOCAL RESTAURANTS: Plaisance, St. Emilion; Amat at Saint James, Bordeaux

TASTING NOTES

CHATEAU
TROPLONG
MONDOT 1994

Terrific, deep dark
ruby/purple color for a
1994; ripe little red fruits on
nose; full-bodied, voluptuous,
and concentrated on the
palate; strong Merlot
character; a big wine without
being harshly tannic.
Rating ★★★

Michel Rolland, revitalized the winemaking in the 1980s.

In a region where most of the vineyard holdings are less than 25 acres, Troplong Mondot's 75 acres make it one of the most important estates in St. Emilion. The natural potential for making fine wine is obvious. The vineyards, in a single block, face south and southwest, covering the plateau overlooking the commune. The vines are 45 years old on average, the oldest being 90 years old. The yield of grapes they produce is naturally limited due to a combination of the following geological factors: a thick limestone bedrock, a layer of clay soil, and the presence of flint and limestone sediments. All these factors give the wine its splendid, dark-ruby hue and poised concentration of flavor.

The lackluster performance of the Troplong wines before 1985 was due to early harvesting and the use of mechanical harvesters (which cannot make a selection between sound and rotten grapes). With late picking and a return to

harvesting by hand, the quality of the raw material has been transformed. The winery has every high-tech aid. Purists may say that the new Troplong wines are fashioned creations whose deep-colored, voluptuous style is more

Château Troplong Mondot seen from the vineyards.

market than *terroir*-driven, but they undoubtedly give a great deal of pleasure to many consumers who regard wine as a hedonistic rather than intellectual experience.

JOSEPH UMATHUM

St. Undraer Strasse 7132, Frauenkirchen, Austria
Tel: (43-2) 172 2440 Fax: (43-2) 172 21734
Visitors: by appointment

*J*oseph Umathum is the leading grower of the village of Frauenkirchen in the Niesiedler See region that lies southeast of Vienna toward the Hungarian border. The Niesiedler lake (*see*) has a major influence on the local climate, the resultant mild springs, hot summers, and clement falls being highly conducive to growing top-quality grapes. Moreover, the soils of the Umathum vineyard are warm, permeable, and rich in minerals such as manganese, making them particularly suitable for serious red-wine production. St. Laurent, the local grape variety, is a class act similar in aromatic potential and subtle flavor to its distant relative, the Pinot Noir, but often more deeply colored and fuller-bodied than the latter.

FACT BOX

OWNER: Joseph Umathum
WINEMAKER: Joseph Umathum
SIZE OF VINEYARD: 46.25 acres
TOTAL ANNUAL PRODUCTION:
information not available
GRAPE VARIETIES: St. Laurent, Zweigelt
AVERAGE AGE OF VINES: 20 years
PERCENTAGE OF NEW WOOD:
30 percent
BEST RECENT VINTAGE: 1992
BEST DISHES TO MATCH WINES:
roast woodcock, veal in cream-based
sauces

In the vineyards, respect for the environment is paramount. The soils are treated as naturally as possible; grass is left between the vines to encourage wildlife; clusters of grapes are thinned and weak shoots removed to reduce yields; harvesting is by hand. The same meticulous care is evident in the winery,

Joseph Umathum tending his vines.

TASTING NOTES

ST. LAURENT VOM STEIN VINEYARD, UMATHUM, 1992

Deep Victoria plum color, scents of briary fruit, spices, and vanilla, new wood lending a touch of sweetness to the ripe berry flavors—all beautifully judged for, though full, the wine remains refined and long-flavored, in no way overextracted. Outstanding.

Rating ★★★★

mirroring the perfectionist principles followed by the best estates in Bordeaux and Burgundy. Slow fermentations produce subtle, tightly-knit, and well-balanced wines with a real taste of their origins. Umathum's best offering to date, a 1992 St. Laurent from the Vom Stein vineyard, is a very exciting glass of red wine, so much so that at a recent international wine gathering of connoisseurs, it was mistaken for a Ruchottes-Chambertin—*méthode ancienne*, of course.

Joseph Umathum in his cellars.

WARWICK ESTATE

P.O. Box 2, Muldersvlei, 7607, South Africa
Tel: (27-21) 884 4410 Fax: (27-21) 884 4025
Visitors: Monday–Friday 8:30AM–4:00PM

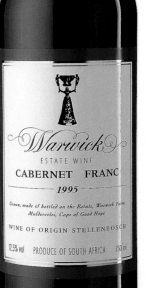

*I*n a beautiful valley between Paarl and Stellenbosch lies Warwick Estate, once part of a vast eighteenth-century farm called "Good Success." The founder of Warwick was Colonel Alexander Gordon, who renamed his portion of the farm in honor of the Warwickshire regiment that he commanded during the Boer War. Like many of his countrymen, he stayed on in South Africa and became a farmer.

Stan Ratcliffe, the present owner, bought Warwick in 1964 with not a vine on the farm. But he had the foresight to plant Cabernet Sauvignon vines that grow so well in this region. With the arrival of his wife Norma in 1971, Stan branched

FACT BOX

OWNERS: Stan and Norma Ratcliffe
WINEMAKER: Norma Ratcliffe
SIZE OF VINEYARD: 87.5 acres
TOTAL ANNUAL PRODUCTION:
15,000 cases
GRAPE VARIETIES: Cabernet Sauvignon, Merlot, Cabernet Franc
PERCENTAGE OF NEW WOOD:
25 percent
BEST RECENT VINTAGE: 1995
BEST DISHES TO MATCH WINES:
roast pheasant, pot-roasted guinea-fowl, steak *au poivre*
LOCAL HOTEL/RESTAURANT:
The Cape Grace Hotel, Cape Town

out from being a successful grape-grower into winemaking.

Norma became an assiduous student of wine and its making. After many trips with Stan to Bordeaux, she decided to build her own cellar and make red wine in the Bordelais style. Merlot and Cabernet Franc were planted in 1980, and by 1985 the vines were in full production. The Ratcliffes prefer old-fashioned methods of red winemaking, crushing the grapes hard in a mechanical press to extract full flavors and tannins. No artificial fining agents are used, and the wine is allowed to settle naturally before being carefully racked. The individual components of the wine are vinified separately and then lodged in 58.5-gallon *barriques* for 9–12 months before the final blend is assembled. In 1986, the Ratcliffes produced "Warwick Trilogy," their first Bordeaux blend in a classic Médoc style. Great stuff, certainly, but their most interesting wine is the Cabernet Franc, brimming with fruit and one of the few successful examples of this pure varietal wine outside France.

> ### TASTING NOTES
>
> #### WARWICK ESTATE CABERNET FRANC 1995
>
> Very deep, lustrous, dark-ruby color, typical of a great year; rich blackberry fruit with hints of spices on nose and palate; mouthfilling ripe tannins, vinous flavors and oak in very good balance. Best vintage to date.
>
> Rating ★★★

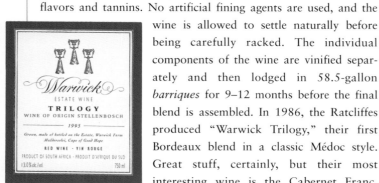

Warwick Estate lies in a valley between Paarl and Stellenbosch.

THE RED WINE *directory*

RISING STARS

Domaine Paul Bruno

Avenida Consistorial 5090, Casila 213, Correo 12
La Reina Penalolen (Santiago) Chile
Tel: (56-2) 284 5470 Fax: (56-2) 284 5469
Visitors: by appointment

*B*ordeaux comes to Chile. In 1990, after six years of observation and research, Bruno Prats, owner of Château Cos d'Estournel, and Paul Pontallier, director of Château Margaux, bought 155 acres of hillside land near Santiago to establish Domaine Paul Bruno, their aim being to create one of the finest red wines of the New World. A third partner, Felipe de Solminihac, a Chilean of French extraction, joined the venture to manage the winery, which trades as Vina Aquitania.

The *domaine* is situated at the foot of the Andes mountains in the area of Quebrada de Macul in the Maipo Valley, which is to Chile what the Haut-Médoc

FACT BOX

OWNER: Vina Aquitania
WINEMAKERS: Bruno Prats, Paul Pontallier, and Felipe de Solminihac
SIZE OF VINEYARD: 155 acres
TOTAL ANNUAL PRODUCTION: 25,000 cases
GRAPE VARIETIES: Cabernet Sauvignon, Merlot
AVERAGE AGE OF VINES: 50 years
PERCENTAGE OF NEW WOOD: 30 percent
BEST RECENT VINTAGES: 1995, 1994
BEST DISHES TO MATCH WINES: navarin of lamb, lightly spiced north Indian dishes

is to Bordeaux. The soil of the vineyard is alluvial, with a top covering of round pebbles that retain the heat of the sun and bring the grapes to maturity. Yet the nights are cool, encouraging a long growing season. The vineyard is planted primarily to Cabernet Sauvignon, with a small proportion of Merlot that will feature in the wines at the time of the new millenium. As elsewhere in Chile, the vines are ungrafted and untreated, apart from minimal sulfuring, thanks to the–as yet–pest-free environment.

> ## TASTING NOTES
> ### DOMAINE PAUL BRUNO CABERNET SAUVIGNON 1995
> Brilliant, youthful, purple ruby; cassis nose with a hint of smokiness; lightly oaked, medium-weight, low key mix of delicious orchard fruit flavors and a touch of mintiness. Excellent.
> Rating ★★★

The goal of the *domaine* is to retain the native charm of Chilean red wines, with their overt fruitiness, while adding greater concentration and ability to age. The grapes are picked by hand and completely destalked, then fermented in stainless steel before 14 days' maceration on the skins. From the 1995 vintage (the second year of production under the new team), the wines are aged in Allier French oak. The essential individuality of the Domaine Paul Bruno style of Cabernet is one in which the tannic structure is disguised by the richness of fruit. In a phrase, they have street appeal *and* a firm backbone–a winning combination, particularly when you want something of enough character to match a fine dish in a restaurant.

CABALLO LOCO

Valdivieso, Lontus, Chile
Not open to the general public

*C*aballo Loco means "crazy horse" in Spanish and is the nickname given to the hyperactive Jorge Cordech, the driving force behind the Valdiviesco wines. This dynamic Chilean enterprise has caught the imagination of the wine world with some superb barrel-aged Cabernet, Merlot, and Pinot Noir Reservas. And now, after years of hard work, Caballo Loco, the winery's prestige *cuvée*, has been released as Valdiviesco's proud statement that South America can run with the best in the world in the red wine stakes.

In order to achieve maximum power with finesse, Caballo Loco has been blended from a range of premium grape varieties (not

FACT BOX

OWNER: Jorge Coderch

WINEMAKERS: Philippe Debrus and Paul Hobbs

SIZE OF VINEYARD: not specified

TOTAL ANNUAL PRODUCTION: 5,000 cases

GRAPE VARIETIES: a blend of premium varieties (unspecified)

AVERAGE AGE OF VINES: 50 years plus

PERCENTAGE OF NEW WOOD: upward of 75 percent

BEST RECENT RELEASES: Caballo Loco No. 1

BEST DISHES TO MATCH WINES: *gigot* of spring lamb with white haricot beans

Owner of Caballo Loco, Jorge Corderch (left).

TASTING NOTES

CABALLO LOCO NUMBER ONE

Deep purple at center of the bowl, gradating to elegant, lustrous ruby at rim; very classy nose, rich in fruit but with considerable complexity; mineral flavors mingle with wood and an impressive vinosity on the palate; very long, silky, and fine. Yes, this is a world-class wine.

Rating ★★★★

specified, but almost certain to include big amounts of Cabernet and Merlot). It is not a wine from a single year but a blend of several top vintages, thus giving the Valdiviesco winemakers complete flexibility to choose only the best. While the wine is certainly drinkable on release, it merits medium- to long-term cellaring. Paul Hobbs, the Californian consultant who also works with Catena (*qv*), and French-born winemaker Philippe Debrus worked together on this new project in 1997, and plan further releases in successive years.

CAPE MENTELLE

P.O. Box 110, Margaret River, Western Australia 6285
Tel: (61-97) 57 32 66 Fax: (61-97) 57 32 33
Visitors: by appointment

*O*f all the rising stars in the New World wine order, David Hohnen must be the dean. An extremely successful Australian winemaker studied who studied viticulture at Davis, California, Hohnen founded the Cape Mentelle vineyards in 1976 with his brother Mark. The Margaret River site proved ideal, for the cool climate of the Indian Ocean and the gravel soils quickly produced some first-rate red wines, particularly Cabernet and Shiraz, of very distinctive fruit and spice characters. Not content to rest on his laurels, Hohnen then purchased the Cloudy Bay vineyard in Marlborough, New Zealand, which, by the late 1980s was setting new standards for Sauvignon Blanc.

FACT BOX

OWNERS: David and Mark Hohnen
WINEMAKER: David Hohnen
SIZE OF VINEYARD: 250 acres
TOTAL ANNUAL PRODUCTION: 30,000 cases
GRAPE VARIETIES: Cabernet Sauvignon, Merlot, Shiraz, Zinfandel
AVERAGE AGE OF VINES: 20 years
PERCENTAGE OF NEW WOOD: upward of 50 percent
BEST RECENT VINTAGES: 1995, 1991
BEST DISHES TO MATCH WINES: grilled and barbecued meats, roast duck

Cape Mentelle reds are made to be eminently drinkable on release. The young Cabernets and Shiraz have exuberant black fruit flavors and lively tannins, but the wines also age beautifully. The 1979 Cabernet Sauvignon still drinks well; with aromas of roasted coffee, black plums and prunes, and a medium weight flavor that has an intriguing finish akin to tawny port. The 1982 Cabernet is outstanding, gloriously full cassis flavors underpinned by supple tannins, and will live well into the next century. The Shiraz has been very successful in recent vintages with a lovely 1993, all briary fruit and wood smoke on the nose, and a rich plum pudding-like flavor, sweet on entry but with a fine dry finish. Hohnen also makes excellent Zinfandel (outstanding 1995 and 1988); suffused with black cherry fruit—there are few wines better with roast duck.

> ## TASTING NOTES
>
> ### CAPE MENTELLE SHIRAZ 1995
>
> Dark ruby purple, near opaque; gorgeous smell and taste of raspberries and plums with a touch of cream; but this is a grown-up wine too, with a serious structure and chewy tannins to ensure an interesting development in bottle over the next ten years. Last tasted January 1998.
> Rating ★★★★

David Hohnen, Managing Director of Cape Mentelle.

CHAMPY PÈRE ET CIE

5 rue du Grenier à Sel, 21202 Beaune
Tel: (33-3) 80 24 92 30 Fax: (33-3) 80 24 97 40
Visitors: daily at 10:30AM

*J*t may seem eccentric to call a venerable old Burgundy house a rising star, but this is a tale with an interesting twist. Champy is almost certainly the oldest *négociant-éleveur* in Beaune, the firm still holding its first 1,720 price lists. A visit here is an antiquarian's delight, thanks to Colonel Merat, a polo-playing cavalryman, who owned the company for much of this century and ensured that the ambience of the Second Empire offices and cellars survived. Quirky touches abound: a double-walled copper cauldron, long used for heating the must in one corner; an 1882 price list

FACT BOX

OWNERS: Henri Meurgey and Associates

WINEMAKER: Michel Ecard

SIZE OF VINEYARD: 15 acres

TOTAL ANNUAL PRODUCTION: 70,000 cases

GRAPE VARIETY: Pinot Noir

AVERAGE AGE OF VINES: 30 years

PERCENTAGE OF NEW WOOD: upward of 30 percent depending on the vintage and wine

BEST RECENT VINTAGES: 1996, 1995, 1993, 1991, 1990

BEST DISHES TO MATCH WINES: breast of Bresse pigeon, free-range chicken

LOCAL RESTAURANT: Le Jardin des Remparts, Beaune

The cellars at Maison Champy.

offering *Richebourg gelé* in another (nothing new, it seems, about cold-soak fermentations); and the *pièce de la résistance*, a vast oak cask converted into a tasting room sporting wall lights shakily inscribed with names to conjure with–Meursault, Volnay, Nuits–pure kitsch. On Merat's death, the firm was purchased by Maison Louis Jadot, who kept the vineyards and sold the firm on to Henri Meurgey, a top Burgundy broker, and his family in 1990.

The Meurgeys have their ears close to the ground. Nobody knows better than they who is currently making the best wines in Burgundy and who is underperforming. Their broking firm, DIVA, handles the export business of 35 of the Côte d'Or's best *domaines* and deals with a further 150 smaller producers. At the end of the 1980s, the family wanted to put a personal stamp on their selections and, when the

The tasting room at Champy, converted from a vast oak cask.

Packaging wines at Champy.

chance came up to buy such a traditional little house as Champy, they jumped at it. The firm is run by Henri's son Pierre, who is as devoted to true Burgundy as his father but has the broader experience of working in computers in his earlier career.

The range of Champy Burgundies offers an authentic expression of the mosaic of different flavors coming from the Côte d'Or. Here Corton tastes like Corton and Gevrey like Gevrey; the wines speak for themselves, not being confined in the straitjacket of a "house style." If there is a common thread at Champy, it is the deft, light touch in the winemaking, which draws out the lovely aromas and the poised silken flavors of classic red Burgundy —at its best the most exciting red wine in the world. A four-hour session tasting a selection of the 1996 vintage in cask (September 1997) convinced me that Champy has made some very impressive wines from this beautiful and plentiful year.

TASTING NOTES

CORTON BRESSANDES 1995

Clear yet vivid cherry color, very Pinot; obviously very young with a long life ahead, but already pure-flavored, frank, and expressive. The silky texture of this medium weight wine belies a firm grip of ripe tannins and a spiciness to come. Subtly oaked. Elegant. Drink from 2001.
Rating ★★★

BODEGAS PALACIO
DE LA VEGA

31263 Dicastello Navarra, Spain
Tel: (34-48) 52 70 09 Fax: (34-48) 52 73 33
Visitors: by appointment

*T*his *bodegas* combines modern winemaking technology and tradition at the magnificent Neo-Gothic Palacio of the Comtessa de la Vega del Pozo. Located at Dicastillo in the heart of Navarra, the palace dominates the surrounding countryside; its recently established *bodegas* has already won a deserved reputation for fine Navarra wines, made with care and sold at kind prices.

With Bordeaux less than three hours' drive away, it is not surprising that the classic French red grape variety Cabernet Sauvignon should feature so strongly (70 percent) in the grape mix for the Crianza.

FACT BOX

OWNERS: Inversiones Arnotegul, S.L.

WINEMAKER: Alicia Eyaralar

SIZE OF VINEYARD: 750 acres

TOTAL ANNUAL PRODUCTION: 100,000 cases

GRAPE VARIETIES: Cabernet Sauvignon, Merlot, Tempranillo, Chardonnay

AVERAGE AGE OF VINES: information not available

PERCENTAGE OF NEW WOOD: upward of 50 percent (American and French oak)

BEST RECENT VINTAGE: 1994

BEST DISHES TO MATCH WINES: roast turkey, spicy lamb, ewe's milk cheese

Softened and refined by 30 percent Tempranillo, this red wine is a winner in the middle price range (under $10 a bottle); gentle enough to drink with roast turkey, it also has enough character for a spicy lamb dish or a pungent ewe's milk cheese. The grapes come from the limestone/gravel soils of the Ribera Alta and Tierra Estella. Fermented in stainless steel for 10 days, the wine is then aged in American oak for 12 months.

The *bodegas* also makes a traditional 100 percent Tempranillo wine of intense berry fruit flavors, a rich and plummy Merlot aged in French oak, and an attractive balanced Chardonnay with a marked citrus and apple character.

> ### TASTING NOTES
>
> #### PALACIO DE LA VEGA CRIANZA 1994
>
> Good rich medium-deep ruby; very respectable bouquet of little red fruits and touches of sweet oak; crowd pleasing full softness initially on palate but underpinned by fine tannins. This wine will continue to drink well until 2000.
> Excellent value.
>
> Rating ★★★

CHATEAU DU CEDRE

Bru, 46700 Vire sur Lot, France
Tel: (33-5) 65 36 53 87 Fax: (33-5) 65 24 64 36
Visitors: by appointment Monday–Friday 10:00AM–4:00PM

*T*he strong red wine of Cahors has a great reputation, just the sort of thing to accompany a steaming *pot au feu* on a cold winter's night. Pascale and Jean Marc Verhaeghe, oenologists and *vignerons*, make the best example I know of at this Vire sur Lot property founded by their grandfather. The vineyard was replanted little by little after the devastating frosts of 1956 and today flourishes on the hillsides of "Bru." This site has the two best types of soil (stony limestone/clay and red sandstone) in the Cahors *appellation*–all very different from the flatlands below, which produce thin, weedy wine.

FACT BOX

OWNERS: Pascale and Jean Marc Verhaeghe
WINEMAKER: Pascale Verhaeghe
SIZE OF VINEYARD: 62.5 acres
TOTAL ANNUAL PRODUCTION: 12,000 cases
GRAPE VARIETIES: Malbec 80 percent, Merlot 10 percent, Tannat 10 percent
AVERAGE AGE OF VINES: 25 years
PERCENTAGE OF NEW WOOD: about 33 percent
BEST RECENT VINTAGES: 1994, 1993
BEST DISHES TO MATCH WINES: *Pot au feu,* jugged hare, strong aged cheeses
LOCAL RESTAURANTS: Le Balance, Cahors; Le Pont del'Ousse, La Cave

The Cuvée Prestige sourced from 32.5 acres of vines of more than 20 years average age is composed of 90 percent Malbec and 10 percent Tannat. Winemaking is very traditional, with total destalking of the grapes, harvesting by hand, high fermentation temperatures of up to 89.6°F, and long vatting times of up to one month. Old procedures such as punching down the cap of fermenting skins are practiced. All these factors allied to the restricted yields contribute to a majestic red wine, powerful but supple, that ages well for 10 to 15 years. Of recent vintages, the 1993, firm and durable, and the 1994, sumptuous and complex, were very successful. They are very good value, too, when compared with great Bordeaux or Rhône wines. The brothers also make a delicious white wine from the Viognier grape.

TASTING NOTES

CAHORS CUVEE PRESTIGE 1994

Magnificent color, sustained, deep shimmering ruby; superb nose, expressive black fruits, a note of tar, in perfect balance with the oak; full and powerful on the palate, supple tannins, an austere end note making an ideal contrast to richly flavored dishes. Outstanding.
Rating ★★★★

ECHEVERRIA

Avenue Amerio Vespucio Norte 568,
Las Condes, Santiago, Chile
Tel: (56-2) 207 43 27 Fax: (56-2) 207 43 28
Visitors: by appointment

*S*uppliers of grapes and wines in bulk to leading Chilean wine producers for much of the twentieth century, the Echeverria family began estate-bottling their finest wines in 1992, mainly for the export market. This very serious firm attaches great importance to quality control at every stage of the wine production process, giving priority to careful vineyard management and precise timing of harvest dates.

The winery is located on the outskirts of Molina in Chile's Central Valley, 120 miles south of Santiago. The 187.5-acre vineyard, half of which is planted with Cabernet Sauvignon, is sited in a single block, making for homogeneity of style and quality. The soils

FACT BOX

OWNER: Echeverria family
WINEMAKER: Echeveria family
SIZE OF VINEYARD: 187.5 acres
TOTAL ANNUAL PRODUCTION:
8,500 cases
GRAPE VARIETY: Cabernet Sauvignon
AVERAGE AGE OF VINES: 50 years
PERCENTAGE OF NEW WOOD:
40 percent
BEST RECENT VINTAGE: 1996
BEST DISHES TO MATCH WINES:
roasted white meats, grilled beef, game
in red wine-based casseroles

THE RED WINE directory

are loam and clay of medium to low fertility, with a well-drained, gravelly subsoil. The climate is Mediterranean, with beneficially big temperature differences of up to 68°F between day and night. The grapes are harvested 100 percent by hand and gently placed in small 30-pound boxes before being transported the very short distance to the winery. The Cabernet "musts" are fermented for seven to 10 days in 7,800-gallon oak tuns before extended skin contact of a further two weeks. The wines are aged in 58.5-gallon French oak barrels for 24 months and, finally, given eight months bottle age before release.

> ### TASTING NOTES
>
> #### ECHEVERRIA
> #### CABERNET
> #### SAUVIGNON
> #### FAMILY RESERVE
> #### 1993
>
> Lovely rich and bright ruby, inviting nose of cassis and cream, exquisite silken texture and a gloriously pure multitoned flavor, delicate yet very persistent. Tasted blind, one might easily confuse this wine with a fine Burgundy or Rioja Alta, though the cassis character is very Cabernet.
>
> Rating ★★★★

This meticulous perfectionist winemaking shows in the glass. The Echeverria Cabernet Sauvignon Family Reserve 1993 is a world-class wine of silken flavors and real complexity, one of the nicest tasting surprises I experienced while researching this book.

Old Cabernet Sauvignon vines in Chile.

BODEGAS ESMERALDA

Guatemala 4565, C.P. 1425 Buenos Aires, Argentina
Tel: (054-1) 833 2080 Fax: (054-1) 832 3086
Visitors to Mendoza vineyards: by appointment

*D*r. Nicolas Catena, scion of an old Mendoza wine family and owner of Bodegas Esmeralda, is one of the pioneering figures in the Argentine wine industry. In the 1970s he led the market in the sale of inexpensive wines for daily drinking. During the last two decades he has been a catalyst for change, striving to make Cabernet Sauvignon, Malbec, and Chardonnay in Mendoza to match the best of California and the Old World.

Teaming up in 1988 with Paul Hobbs, the gifted winemaker at Simi estate in California, Catena discovered that Mendoza Cabernets possess great complexity, intensity of aroma, and considerable elegance of flavor. He also came to believe

FACT BOX

OWNER: Dr. Nicolas Catena
WINEMAKER: José Galanté
SIZE OF VINEYARD: 450 acres
TOTAL ANNUAL PRODUCTION: 20,000 cases
GRAPE VARIETY: Cabernet Sauvignon
AVERAGE AGE OF VINES: 15 years
PERCENTAGE OF NEW WOOD: upward of 50 percent
BEST RECENT VINTAGES: 1995, 1991
BEST DISHES TO MATCH WINES: barbecued meats, stews, casseroles, and strong cheeses

Agrelo vineyard at Bodegas Esmeralda.

that given low yields, his prime Agrelo vineyard could produce wines that aged like a good Bordeaux or Napa Valley premium red. The problem was that the image of Argentine wine was associated with cheap jug wine costing $4 a bottle. He was advised that he had to make a Cabernet that tasted like a $25 California wine but that sold for $15. And that is exactly what he did. The 1991 Catena Cabernet was released at this keen price to excellent notices from the wine press.

TASTING NOTES

ALAMOS RIDGE CABERNET SAUVIGNON 1995

Dramatic, inviting color, deep Victoria plum with mauve highlights, gives a hint of the wine's vigor; hot country nose, "blind" it could be something grand from the southern Rhône, intense brambly smells of cooked fruits (plums, blackberries); full, seamless flavors on the palate, forward and well rounded but with a nice tannic grip as an end note. Excellent value.

Rating ★★★★

More recently, Catena has released the Alamos Ridge Cabernet Sauvignon, which sells for under $10 and represents one of the best wine values in the world. Both wines are made to the highest standards from grape to glass. The harvest is handpicked, the fermented wines stay on the skins for a month and are then aged in top-quality French oak barrels for nine months, bottled, and rested for a further two to three years before release. What more can you ask at these prices?

Winemaker Jose Galante.

TIM GRAMP WINES

Mintaro Road, Watervale, South Australia 5452
Tel: (61-8) 84 31 33 38 Fax: (61-8) 84 31 32 29
Visitors: weekdays and public holidays 10:30AM–4:30PM

With just five acres of his own mature vines and careful purchasing of fruit from a couple of grape growers in the Southern Vales, Tim Gramp is one of the best small producers in Australia making wines with a character the big producers only dream about. In 1996 I was stopped in my tracks by his succulent warm flavored McLaren Vale Grenache, as good as any wine from this grape that I have tasted outside the Rhône valley and frankly a lot better than much within it.

Gramp makes an excellent Cabernet Sauvignon from his own 20-year-old vines

FACT BOX

OWNER: Tim Gramp

WINEMAKER: Tim Gramp

SIZE OF VINEYARD: 5 acres

TOTAL ANNUAL PRODUCTION: 55 tons

GRAPE VARIETIES: Grenache, Shiraz, Cabernet Sauvignon

AVERAGE AGE OF VINES: 20 years

PERCENTAGE OF NEW WOOD: 80 percent (for Cabernet Sauvignon and Shiraz)

BEST RECENT VINTAGES: 1996, 1994

BEST DISHES TO MATCH WINES: Thai duck with red curry paste (Grenache)

LOCAL RESTAURANT: Mintaro Mews, Mintaro

TASTING NOTES

McCLAREN VALE GRENACHE 1996

Shimmering mid-toned ruby, a very natural color suggesting a proper fine wine; lovely warm country Grenache fruit expression on nose and palate, juicy and very approachable on entry; complexities of spice and a little charred oak on middle palate hold the interest beyond the obvious deliciousness of the fruit. A captivating wine for all seasons. Will hold well until 1999.

Rating ★★★★

and fine Shiraz too from bought-in fruit. The reds ferment to dryness on the skins in 7-ton open fermenters–both the Shiraz and the Cabernet Sauvignon are aged in American oak barrels. Gramp's wines were first exported to Malaysia but are now available in Britain from Adnams of Southwold. Drink the Grenache with Thai duck and red curry paste for a gastronomic match made in heaven!

TENUTA DELL'ORNELLAIA

Via Bolgherese 191, 57020, Italy
Tel: (39-565) 76 21 40 Fax: (39-565) 76 21 44
Visitors: by appointment only

*L*odovico Antinori was born with a head start in life. The Antinoris have been an integral part of the merchant nobility of Florence since 1385 when they joined the Vintners Guild in their city. And at least one member of the family has worked in the wine trade in any given period since that date. The family's landed estates in Tuscany were greatly extended during the eighteenth and nineteenth centuries and considerable winemaking experience was also acquired. An important negoçiant firm was founded at the beginning of the twentieth century.

FACT BOX

OWNER: Marchese Lodovico Antinori

WINEMAKER: Tibor Ga'l

SIZE OF VINEYARD: 337.5 acres

TOTAL ANNUAL PRODUCTION: 29,000 cases (but only 1,500 cases of Masseto)

GRAPE VARIETIES: Cabernet Sauvignon 42 percent; Merlot 40 percent; Cabernet Franc 5 percent; remainder Sauvignon Blanc

AVERAGE AGE OF VINES: 35 years

PERCENTAGE OF NEW WOOD: Ornellaia 33 percent; Masseto 100 percent

BEST RECENT VINTAGES: 1995, 1993, 1990

BEST DISHES TO MATCH WINES: game, roasts, lamb, pheasant, cheeses

LOCAL RESTAURANTS: La Pineta, Scacciapensieri, Gambero Rosso

Marchese Lodovici worked in the family business for a while, but being something of a loner decided to go his own way and in the early 1980s planted an extensive vineyard at Tenuta dell'Ornellaia, a family estate at Bolgheri on the Mediterranean coast, 60 miles from Florence. This part of the Maremma, apart from being one of the most wildly beautiful places on earth, is a rich agricultural area, a zone with an important winemaking potential. Lodovico's uncle, Marchese Incisa della Rochetta, brought the wine world's attention to Bolgheri with his pioneering work at Tenuta San Guido and the creation of the Cabernet-led Sassiciaia (*qv*), now recognized as one of the great red wines of the world.

Lodovico Antinori has followed Incisa's example at next door Ornellaia, though the range and style of the wines is quite different. After consulting international viticultural and winemaking authorities, men like Michel Rolland and Danny Schuster, it was quite clear to Antinori that the character of the Bolgheri soils were similar to those of St.-Emilion and Pomerol in Bordeaux and ideal for the production of fine red wine. The originality of the Ornellaia vineyard in an Italian context is the significant presence of Merlot. Although representing an important part (40 percent) of the assemblage for the flagship red wine, Ornellaia, Merlot reaches its apogee in the "Vigna Vecchia" (old vines) sector of the estate. Since 1987, this parcel has provided the raw material for a 100 percent Merlot cuvée called Masseto. For my money, this is the most interesting and distinctive wine in the cellar. The 1993 (*see* Tasting Notes) is a splendid success. The grapes were picked under sunny September skies. After a prolonged maceration of 18–20 days, the wine was allowed to decant naturally in tank before being put into new *barriques* for an eventual two years of aging. The result is a structured wine of great purity of fruit and beautiful balance.

TASTING NOTES

MASSETO 1993

Deep youthful violet red; great purity of primary Merlot aromas; beautifully balanced flavor, a hint of licorice, the oak finely integrated. Very persistent finish. Class.

Rating ★★★★

CHATEAU PHELAN SEGUR

33180 St. Estèphe, France
Tel: (33-5) 56 59 30 09 Fax: (33-5) 56 59 30 04
Visitors: by appointment only

*P*hélan Ségur, a very handsome, early nine-teenth-century manor house, lies in a high position at the southern end of St. Estèphe overlooking the Gironde Estuary. The original property was the creation of Frank Phélan, an Irish businessman who emigrated to Bordeaux to become a wine grower. The complete architectural integration of the château and the farm buildings that house the cellars is eloquent testimony to one man's vision of an idyllic wine estate.

FACT BOX

OWNER: Xavier Gardinier
WINEMAKER: Thierry Gardinier
SIZE OF VINEYARD: 162.5 acres
SECOND LABEL: Frank Phélan
TOTAL ANNUAL PRODUCTION:
25,000 cases
GRAPE VARIETIES: Cabernet Sauvignon
60 percent; Merlot 35 percent; Cabernet
Franc 5 percent
AVERAGE AGE OF VINES: 30 years
PERCENTAGE OF NEW WOOD:
up to 50 percent
BEST RECENT VINTAGES: 1996, 1995,
1990, 1989
BEST DISHES TO MATCH WINES:
beef, lamb, game
LOCAL HOTEL AND RESTAURANT:
Château Cordeillan-Bages, Hotel de
France et de l'Angleterre; both in
Pauillac

The property went through a very bad period during the early 1980s and was sold by the Delon family to Xavier Gardinier, the former head of Champagne Pommery, in 1985. Very much a man in the Frank Phélan mold, Gardinier placed a firm reforming hand on the wine operation from the start. Faced with several vintages (1982– 1985) that had tainted chemical aromas, he promptly removed them from sale and sued a well-known manufacturer of herbicides, alleging that it was these products that had caused the problem.

> ## TASTING NOTES
>
> ### CHATEAU PHELAN SEGUR 1995
>
> Deep, rich, ruby color; elegant and vivid, not crudely extracted; lovely cassis and spices on nose; medium weight, supple, "*gras*," great charm, ripe bolstering tannins. A complete wine.
> Rating ★★★

The estate has since been completely restored and is now on the way to realizing its potential as one of the finest wines of St. Estèphe. The vineyard, situated on predominantly sandy soils between Montrose and Calon Ségur, produces grapes with a particularly refined and supple flavor. The good age of the vines (some 60 years old) adds depth and complexity. Indeed, the Bordeaux oenologist who advises the estate calls Phélan-Ségur the St. Julien of St. Estèphe.

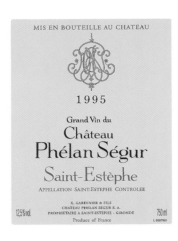

MIS EN BOUTEILLE AU CHATEAU

1995

Grand Vin du
Château
Phélan Ségur
Saint-Estèphe
APPELLATION SAINT-ESTEPHE CONTROLEE

X. GARDINIER & FILS
CHATEAU PHELAN SEGUR S. A.
PROPRIETAIRE A SAINT-ESTEPHE · GIRONDE
Produce of France

12.5%vol.   750 ml

Thierry Gardinier, Xavier's son, makes the wine with a vigilant eye for detail at every stage from grape to glass. The land is tilled according to traditional methods, manual labor being preferred to modern methods of weed removal. Yields are restricted; grapes are harvested by hand into small baskets, and on arrival at the presshouse they are individually sorted on a conveyor to eliminate any that are rotten. Fermentation takes place in small stainless-steel tanks in order to allow the three separate root stocks (Cabernet Sauvignon, Merlot, and Cabernet Franc) to be stored separately by origin and age. The traditional Bordelais method of pumping over the fermenting wine to moisten the cap of grape skins is used only sparingly at Phélan, since Thierry believes that this process accentuates harsh tannins in the finished wine. No filtration is used before barrelling, and there is only a light filtration before bottling.

Since the 1987 vintage, the Gardiniers have not put a foot wrong. The trio of 1988, 1989, and 1990 are top-flight efforts, the 1991 is a softly textured but well-structured marvel, and the impressively fruity 1992 shows what can be done by strict grape selection in a rain-sodden year. The succulent and charming 1995 precedes what promises to be an outstanding 1996, all rich, chewy flavors of perfectly ripe Cabernet. At an opening price of under $29 a bottle, it may be the buy of the vintage and terrific value for money.

Château Phelan Segur overlooking the Gironde
Estuary in St. Estephe

LE PIN

33500 Pomerol, France
Tel: (33-5) 57 51 33 99 Fax: (33-5) 57 25 35 08
Visitors: not open to the general public

*T*his may be the most expensive claret in Bordeaux, but it can hardly be pigeonholed as a classic as its first vintage was in 1979. Also, the more staid of wine commentators drone on about the strong oak flavors masking the wine. I find these criticisms literally sour grapes in the mouths of jealous competitors who are unable to achieve Le Pin's stratospheric prices. In my opinion, the wines show an astounding level of consistency, vintage after vin-

tage. During fermentation, the wines are allowed to go as high as 89.6°F, which explains the rich, supple *gras* texture and flavor, allied, of course, to low yields. The average production is a minuscule 600 cases for all world markets.

The early vintages are showing beautifully now, with a fine complex 1982, a beautifully balanced 1983, and a highly exotic 1989.

The 1990 and 1996 are the two great wines of the current decade. Very different in style, the 1990 is voluptuous, smooth, and attractive, while the 1996 is very concentrated.

FACT BOX

OWNER: Jacques Thienpont
WINEMAKERS: Thienpoint family
SIZE OF VINEYARD: 5 acres
TOTAL ANNUAL PRODUCTION: 600 cases
GRAPE VARIETIES: Cabernet Sauvignon 90 percent; Merlot 10 percent
AVERAGE AGE OF VINES: 18 years
PERCENTAGE OF NEW WOOD: 100 percent
BEST RECENT VINTAGES: 1996, 1990, 1989, 1986, 1983
BEST DISHES TO MATCH WINES: beef, lamb, and game
LOCAL RESTAURANT: Plaisance, St. Emilion

St. Helena Wine Estate

Coutts Island Road, P.O. Box 1, Belfast, New Zealand
Tel: (64-3) 323 8202 Fax: (64-3) 323 8252
Visitors: by appointment

*T*his estate has shown the world that New Zealand is one of the few places outside Burgundy where Pinot Noir can be grown successfully and made into an aromatic and elegant wine worthy of the name. Located just north of Christchurch on the Canterbury Plains, the vineyard was planted in 1978 on the land of horticulturalists Robin and Norman Mundy who used to grow potatoes here. In their early years the Mundys had the good luck to be advised by Danny Schuster, one of the world's great viticulturalists, who was also the winemaker for a while. The 1982 vintage of Pinot Noir received rave notices for its fragrance, poise, and structure—a real alternative to red

FACT BOX

OWNERS: Robin and Bernice Mundy
WINEMAKER: Petter Evans
SIZE OF VINEYARD: 50 acres
TOTAL ANNUAL PRODUCTION: 9,000 cases
GRAPE VARIETY: Pinot Noir
AVERAGE AGE OF VINES: 20 years
PERCENTAGE OF NEW WOOD: upward of 33 percent
BEST RECENT VINTAGES: 1996, 1995, 1991, 1988
BEST DISHES TO MATCH WINES: game and red meats

St. Helena Estate Pinot Noir 1996

Fine, bright and clear ruby with vermilion tints; ripe cherry and plum aromas; confirming richness and weight on the palate but with the beautiful balance and silky mouthfeel a lover of Pinot Noir looks for before all else.

Rating ★★★

Burgundy. The Canterbury area was clearly a hospitable home to the temperamental grape; the South Island summers were long, fall was dry, and the soils rich in limestone.

Robin Mundy is now a full time *vigneron* and runs the estate with his wife Bernice. The current winemaker, Petter Evans, is a worthy successor to the great Schuster. A graduate of Roseworthy Agricultural College, Australia–the Davis of the southern hemisphere–Evans ferments his Pinot Noir on the skins for an average of 15 days and then matures the wine in French oak barrels for a year. Very successful Pinot Noir wines were made in 1988 and 1991 and both the 1995 and 1996 look promising. St. Helena is one of the very few New Zealand wineries producing Pinot Gris (one detects the influence of Danny Schuster); it is a delicate floral white with a long dry finish.

St. Helena

CANTERBURY
PINOT NOIR 1996

Produced & Bottled by St Helena Wine Estate
Coutts Island Rd Christchurch
PRODUCE OF NEW ZEALAND
13% vol.   e 75cl

Robin Mundy, *vigneron*, and his wife Bernice.

VERGELEGEN

P.O. Box 17, Somerest West, 7129 South Africa
Tel: (27-21) 847 1334 Fax: (27-21) 847 1606
*Visitors: daily 9:30am–3:00pm except
Good Friday and Christmas Day*

*V*ergelegen means "situated far away," and there is certainly a timeless, dreamy quality about this exquisite Cape Dutch estate whose history closely shadows that of the first Dutch and Huguenot settlers in South Africa. Its first owner, Willem Adrianne van der Stel, was granted the estate in 1700 when he became governor of the Cape in succession to his father, Simon van der Stel.

Willem Adrienne was a Renaissance man. In his six short years at Vergelegen, he put his knowledge as a botanist, forester, and horticulturalist to lasting effect; half a million vines were planted, 18 cattle stations were established, camphors and

FACT BOX

OWNERS: Anglo American Farms Ltd.

WINEMAKER: Martin Meinert

SIZE OF VINEYARD: 257.5 acres

TOTAL ANNUAL PRODUCTION: 40,000 cases

GRAPE VARIETIES: Cabernet Sauvignon, Merlot, Cabernet Franc

PERCENTAGE OF NEW WOOD: 10 percent (American oak)

BEST RECENT VINTAGES: 1997, 1995

BEST DISHES TO MATCH WINES: ragout of rabbit and oyster mushrooms

RESTAURANT: Lady Phillips

The majestic Table Mountain provides a sweeping
backdrop to the Vergelegen winery.

oaks were set in the ground. But the scale and speedy realization of
his vision had made him enemies, and in 1806, he was dismissed by
the directors of the Dutch East Company and returned to the
Netherlands.

Vergelegen passed through a succession of owners over the
next 200 years. The Theunissen family, who owned the estate from
1798 until 1899, maintained the vineyards. The estate then
declined until it was bought in 1917 by Sir Lionel Phillips, one
of the "Rand Lords," who had made
an immense fortune from diamond
prospecting in Kimberley. His wife,
Lady Florence, restored the homestead
and gardens and spend vast sums on
the estate itself. But she also decided to
pull up all the vines, converting the
land to mixed farming.

In 1987, a company formed as a
joint venture of the Anglo American
Corporation and De Beers, bought
Vergelegen. One of the main projects
undertaken was the replanting of the

vineyards which, by 1997, extended to 257.5 acres in production. All the red wines are made from the estate's own grapes. Cabernet Sauvignon is the flagship grape variety, accounting for nearly a third of the vines. Merlot is also an important varietal, and there are much smaller plantings of Cabernet Franc and Sangiovese (Chardonnay and Sauvignon Blanc are grown, too).

High on a hill above False Bay, the state-of-the-art winery is a striking octagonal building designed by the Paris-based architects Patrick Dillon and Jean de Castines, whose previous work has included the second-year *chai* at Château Lafite-Rothschild in Pauillac. Martin Meinert, Vergelegen's winemaker, worked at Lafite during the 1992 harvest, which resulted in a close relationship with Gilbert Rokvam, Lafite's technical director. In a reciprocal visit, Gilbert observed and advised on the 1993 vintage at Vergelegen.

The gentlest handling of the grapes and infant wine is the guiding principle of Vergelegen winemaking, a gravity system operating with the harvest reception bay situated above the press which, in turn, is sited above the barrels. The style of the red wines is fruity and soft enough to give immediate pleasure on release, but also has sufficient complexity, structure, elegance, and balance to age interestingly. The 1995 Vergelegen Cabernet Sauvignon has been a spectacular success, winning a gold medal at the International Wine Challenge in London on its first outing. Peer into the crystal ball to 2025 and the by-then mature vines might be producing a mini-Lafite at the southern tip of Africa.

DOMAINE ROSSIGNOL-TRAPET

Rue de la Petite Issue, 21220 Grevrey-Chambertin, France
Tel: (33-3) 80 51 87 26 Fax: (33-3) 80 34 31 63
Visitors: by appointment only, open all year
9:00AM–12 NOON and 2:00PM–6:00PM

*T*his estate was created in 1990 following the division of the old *Domaine* Louis Trapet between Jean Trapet and his sister Mado, wife of Jacques Rossignol of Volnay. The welcome from this smiling family of *vignerons* is warm and very Burgundian.

Nicolas and David, Jacques' sons, are breathing new life into the Trapet name, which had become somewhat tarnished by lackluster wines made here in the 1980s. Nicolas, a graduate of the prestigious wine school in Toulouse, is a winemaker with a light touch who knows that great red Burgundy is all about the subtlety of lingering, succulent

FACT BOX

OWNERS: Rossignol-Trapet family
WINEMAKER: Nicolas Rossignol
SIZE OF VINEYARD: 35 acres
TOTAL ANNUAL PRODUCTION: 6,000 cases
GRAPE VARIETIES: Pinot Noir 95 percent; Chardonnay 5 percent
AVERAGE AGE OF VINES: 40 years
PERCENTAGE OF NEW WOOD: 25–30 percent
BEST RECENT VINTAGES: 1996, 1995, 1993
LOCAL RESTAURANTS: Moulin aux Canards, Aubigny; Vendanges de Bourgogne, Gevrey

flavors, not the ramrod punch of alcoholic power. Pinot Noir in Burgundy, he says, is like a hand in a velvet glove, as it is the soil that fashions its character. Harvesting by hand is absolutely essential, since only a gentle treatment of the vine allows it to live a long life. The vine stock itself must be healthy and virus-free, for how can a vine with a cold perform properly?

The *domaine* employs classical vinification methods, with partial destalking of the grapes and a vatting time of 14–16 days. The Rossignols think it essential to taste the fermenting must every day in order to determine the best time to stop fermentation. Like all great Burgundy makers, their goal is to give full expression to their exceptional *terroirs*, which include prime sites in Chambertin, Latricières-Chambertin, Chapelle-Chambertin, and Beaune *premier cru* Teurons. Their holding in Morey St. Denis *Rue de Vergy* produces excellent, aromatic, and quite forward red Burgundy at a kind price. (The 1992 was a triumph in a patchy year.)

> ## TASTING NOTES
> ### LATRICIERES-CHAMBERTIN 1995
> When first opened color was a light vermillion, the sort of hue that puts off critics inexperienced in tasting great red Burgundy; yet over three days in a stoppered bottle, the color of this lovely wine perceptible deepened; exquisitely delicate bouquet typical of Latricières; wonderful balance, length and completeness on palate. A very great wine made with a light touch.
> Rating ★★★★★

The family firmly believes that the use of new wood should be subtle because "Pinot Noir is a very aromatic grape and cannot support too much oak. That's why we use only 25 percent new wood for our Villages wines and 33 percent for our *premiers crus*; for our *grands crus*, such as Le Chambertin, that proportion may be as much as 50 percent."

The classic 1993 vintage at Rossignol–Trapet was particularly successful, and 1995 was a challenging vintage for the winemaker where a light touch was essential to bring out all the aromatics and finesse from healthy, ripe, but concentrated and tannic grapes. Nicolas was well up to the test, his exquisite 1995 Latricières the striking proof. This is a *domaine* on its way back to the top.

VINTAGE CHART

*V*intage charts are no more than a rough gauge of the sort of quality to expect in any given year–with many exceptions. Moreover, in the southern hemisphere, especially the hotter vineyards of Chile, South Africa, and Australia, vintage variations are less marked.

However, a vintage guide is useful for the classic red wines of France, Italy, and Spain; also those of California. The variable weather at the all important time of early September, just before the harvest, is a critical factor that affects the quality of the vintage.

Region Year	96	95	94	93	92	91	90	89	88	87	86	85	84	83	82	81	80	79	78	77	76	75	74
Claret	**17**	**16**	15	14	12	13	19	18	18	*14*	18	16	*12*	15	20	15	–	16	14	–	15	16	–
Burgundy	**18**	**18**	15	**19**	14	17	**20**	17	18	15	13	17	–	15	13	15	–	16	18	–	16	8	–
Rhône	**17**	**18**	17	14	14	16	**18**	18	17	–	16	17	–	*17*	16	19	–	16	20	–	–	–	–
Piedmont	**17**	**18**	**16**	**15**	**15**	**14**	**18**	16	18	–	17	18	–	17	*15*	16	–	16	20	–	–	–	–
Tuscany	**17**	**19**	16	16	13	15	**19**	*11*	18	–	–	18	–	17	16	17	–	16	20	–	–	–	–
Rioja	**17**	**17**	**19**	16	14	15	16	17	14	*18*	*14*	17	–	–	20	–	–	16	–	–	–	–	–
Ribeiro del Duero	**17**	**18**	**18**	16	15	13	**20**	**17**	15	15	*14*	16	–	–	18	19	–	–	–	–	17	17	–
California	**19**	**18**	**19**	**17**	18	18	18	*12*	*15*	17	*15*	18	–	–	14	–	16	–	15	16	–	–	18

KEY

Numbers 1 (the worst) to 20 (the best)

17	**Bold** characters: wine needs to be matured longer
17	Straight character: can be drunk but will improve further
<u>17</u>	<u>Straight character</u> (underlined): ready to drink
17	*Italics*: might still be drinkable but approach with care
–	this vintage is hard to find

GLOSSARY

APPELLATION D'ORIGINE CONTRÔLÉE (AOC): certificate vouching for the authenticity and origin of a fine French wine whose name is printed on the label (for example, Volnay, Pauillac, Côte Rôtie).

ASSEMBLAGE: the assembly or blending of wines from different vats.

BARRIQUE: Bordeaux term for a small oak barrel of about 50 gallons capacity.

CAVE: wine cellar, usually below the ground.

CHAI: Bordeaux name for a wine "cellar" or warehouse, usually at ground level.

CHAPEAU: literally, "hat"; the top of fermenting grapes, usually pips and skins.

CHÂTEAU: a vineyard estate, especially in the Bordeaux region of France.

CLASSIFIED GROWTH: one of the élite vineyard estates of the Médoc (Bordeaux) classified in 1855; usually very expensive.

CLIMAT: a particular vineyard site or growth; term much used in Burgundy.

CRU: growth; often describes a wine, usually of high quality, from a specific vineyard (see also Grand Cru; Premier Cru).

CRU BOURGEOIS: one of the well-regarded Médoc vineyard estates in the category below that of a classified growth; in practice, a top cru bourgeois can make superb wine.

CUVE: a vat or tank used for fermenting grapes into wine.

CUVÉE: after blending, the final finished wine; téte de cuvée designates the finest wine a grower makes.

CÔTE: slope; when used to identify a wine, as in Côtes de Nuits, the term usually signifies the basic generic quality of the wine grown in that district.

CÔTEAU: hillside.

DÉBOURBAGE: decanting or cleansing process of pressed juice prior to fermentation.

DEMI-MUID: an oak cask 132 gallons capacity.

DOC/DOCG: Italian equivalent of French AOC vouching for the authenticity of named wine.

DOMAINE: a vineyard estate, especially in the Burgundy region of France.

ÉGRAPPAGE: the destalking of grapes prior to fermentation.

FOUDRE: large wooden cask of no fixed size.

GAMEY: tasting term used to describe aromas and flavors akin to game birds and other animals; implies pungency and maturity of taste; very characteristic of aged red Burgundy.

GENERIC: word for a wine of the most basic standard of AOC, for example Bourgogne Rouge, Beaujolais, Côtes du Rhône.

GRAND CRU: great growth–the highest classification, especially in Burgundy for the top vineyard sites.

GOÛT DE TERROIR: taste of the earth, in its quasi-mythical and rather vague translation. More practically, used to describe a wine (probably a great one) whose flavor is deep, complex, concentrated, with hints of minerals derived from the soil of the vineyard.

GRAS: literally "fat," a round supple fullness of texture and flavor in a fine wine.

HECTARE (HA.): 2.47 acres.

HECTOLITER: 100 litres/approx. 22 gallons.

LEES: sediment–the byproducts of fermentation–that falls to the floor of the tank during the wine-making process.

LIEU-DIT: the name of a particular vineyard site, often of folkloric origin (for example, Les Amoureuses/ "Women in love" site in Chambolle-Musigny).

MALOLACTIC FERMENTATION: conversions of malic acid into

milder lactic acid in order to make the wine softer, rounder, but also more complex.

MAITRE DE CHAI: cellar-master (Bordeaux).

MONOPOLE: a word used in Burgundy for a wine estate or named site under single ownership (for example, Clos de Tart, Romanée Conti).

MUST: grape juice and matter before and during fermentation; after which it becomes a young wine.

NEGOCIANT: stockholder, merchant shipper and exporter of wine.

NÉGOCIANT-ÉLEVEUR: stockholder/merchant who buys in grapes then often makes them into wine, which he tends and matures before sale.

PARCELLE: parcel. A plot of land or row of vines within a wine estate.

PIGEAGE: punching-down of the black or red grape skins below the surface of the wine during fermentation in order to deepen the color and judiciously maximize the extract in the wine.

PREMIER CRU: first growth. In Bordeaux applies to a handful of top wine estates; in Burgundy refers, confusingly, to so-called second-rank vineyards below those designated grands crus.

PRIMEUR: word used to describe a wine that is sold young; generally attractive to drink within a few months of the vintage. Term also used in Bordeaux for claret bought young in the "futures" market.

REMONTAGE: the vigorous pumping-over of young fermenting wine in order to extract maximum color, extract and tannins; a cruder method than pigeage.

SULPHUR DIOXIDE (SO2): dissolved disinfecting gas/chemical used to protect wine and prevent biological spoilage. Overdone, it can make a wine unpalatable and headache-making.

VIGNERON: wine grower.

VINE DE GARDE: a wine that needs to be kept and matured, often for a decade, in order to develop the full complexities of its flavors.

INDEX

ACKNOWLEDGEMENTS

The publishers would like to thank all those who helped in the preparation
of this book.
Page 7, 27 e.t. archive; pages 9, 10 H. Roger Viollet; page 14 Pichon Longueville
Comtesse de Lalande; pages 15, 23, 25, 31, 32, 33, 34, 35, 37, 38, 40, 42, 44,
45, 46, 47, 231 Janet Price; page 16 Bodegas Muga; page 20 San Guido Sassicaia;
page 27 Liz Mott; pages 60, 61 (top) Serge Bois-Prevost; pages 69, 70 Gilles
d'Auzac; pages 177, 178 Emma Borg.